MAKING MORE S

8 Top Projects to Enlarge Your Home *with*

Home extensions   Conservatories   Loft conv

Converting Garages, Outbuildings and Basements

Remodelling Internal Layouts

By   Ian Rock MRICS

CW01455318

Dedication

This book is dedicated to the late ***Naomi Handford-Jones***
who originally inspired this subject
as a presentation for the
National Self-build & Renovation Centre

Contents

MAKING MORE SPACE

8 Top Projects to Enlarge Your Home *without spending a fortune*

Introduction

Just imagine what you could do with more space added to your home. Perhaps a fabulous new kitchen/diner or a home office. Maybe a spare bedroom that would be perfect for sleepovers. Or how about a lavishly equipped home cinema or fitness studio? Either way, enlarging your home doesn't have to cost a fortune. Great results can be achieved at a budget price by following some simple rules and picking the option that best suits your property.

There are basically two ways you can go about making more space. The obvious solution is to build out externally, by constructing a new extension, conservatory or a garden office. But you can also transform your home by making the most of the space you've already got - by converting the loft or a garage - or simply by re-modelling the interior layout.

The fact is, any fool can spend a fortune and end up with a mediocre extension. The smart thing is to make the best of your home without wasting a lot of money. The trick is to spend no more than is genuinely necessary. So the ethos of this book is that by keeping the design simple and carefully planning and managing the project, you can create high quality living space at minimal cost.

The book is split into 2 parts. In Part 1 we look at how to pick the solution that suits you best, and how to prepare things in advance to ensure your building project runs smoothly. We also explain which projects need Planning or Building Regulations consent. And before parting with any hard-earned cash, it's interesting to consider how much value different sorts of home improvements can add to your home in relation to their cost. Then in Part 2 we come to the real meat of the subject, exploring 8 ways to enlarge and adapt your home, in each case highlighting the various pros and cons. And for every project we reveal exactly how much you are legally allowed to build without the need for planning permission – you may be surprised at how generous the rules are!

PART 1
Before You Start

1. What adds the most value?

Do you ever wonder which home improvements add the maximum value to a property? Of course the prime motivation for enlarging your home is to improve your lifestyle. But it's nice to know that in most cases you will also be adding to your nest egg.

Spending money to enlarge your property also makes a lot of sense when you consider the alternative. Moving to a bigger house typically costs around £20,000 paid out in fees and taxes alone - money that's effectively flushed away. Most of the projects in this guidebook can be carried out for this sort of financial outlay, and in some cases considerably less!

Homes & Design

'WE'VE ADDED £100,000 TO THE VALUE OF OUR HOME'

Struggling for space? In the current climate, building an extension is the easiest way to give your family room to grow – and add value too. **Graham Norwood** reports

If you want to see why "don't move, improve" is the perfect catchphrase for today's volatile housing market, just ask Nick and Katie White. The couple, who have two children aged two and four,

Changing rooms

■ Always check whether your expansion plans require planning permission – in some cases you can extend by 15 per cent of the original volume of the house without requiring council consent. Check on www.planningportal.gov.uk.

The following research from Nationwide Building Society is fairly typical of the value you can expect improvements to add to a property - although much will depend on the size, quality and specification of the finished result.

Average % value added	
1. Loft conversion	+ 21%
2. Another bedroom	+ 12%
3. Central heating	+ 6.8%
4. Parking	+ 6.5%
5. An extra bathroom	+ 5.2%

Adding a room in the roof is consistently voted one of the best ways to add value – as much as 20% to the price of an average 3 bedroom home. But this sort of data needs to be taken with a pinch of salt, because every location has 'ceiling' prices' above which even the most massively extended house won't figure – so there can be diminishing returns above a certain price level.

Once you've increased the total floor area of your home, the new space may have potential for multiple different uses – some of which add more value for buyers than others. Additional bedrooms and enlarged kitchens usually hit the spot adding the maximum value.

But in reality the key factor to adding value to a specific property is the extent to which you're overcoming an obvious drawback, such as a tiny kitchen.

However, before getting too excited about increasing the value of your home, it helps to have some idea of what a project is likely to cost.

What's it going to cost?

There's only one thing better than discovering that improving your home has massively boosted its value – and that's if the work didn't cost much to do! Then as well as gaining a more spacious home, you should be looking a tidy sum in pure profit.

If you're on a very limited budget it's usually possible to keep costs down by making a major DIY contribution. Some of the projects featured can even be self-built 100%, so in effect you only have to pay for materials. And by cutting out all the labour costs and the builder's profit margin, you would typically paying only about 1/3rd of the price charged by a building contractor.

Here's a rough price guide assuming you paid builders to do the whole thing:-

IMPROVEMENT	Approx £
Loft conversion	1000 to 1800 m2
Extension simple 2 storey brick & block	1500 to 2200 m2
Basement conversion	2000 to 2500 m2
where the floor needs lowering where floor needs lowering	2650 to 3200 m2
excavate new basement	4000 to 5000 m2
Garage conversion	900 to 1300 m2
Removing a load bearing wall	1000 to 1500 per metre run

2. Planning ahead

A badly planned project will inevitably go 'pear-shaped' further down the line. This may make for entertaining TV, but in the real world without the benefit of a celebrity property guru conveniently at hand it can easily turn into a nightmare. One that usually boils down to disputes with builders about money.

Whatever type of project you're considering, the key to success is thinking the job through in advance – checking whether the proposed works will require Planning or Building Regulations consent, finding a good builder and, crucially, drawing up a realistic budget. Time spent at this stage can save a huge amount of heartache and expense later on – after all, it's a lot easier to move a wall on a drawing than it is later on site!

What's the use?
Clearly one of the first things you're going to decide is what the new space is for. The purpose that you want to use your new accommodation for will dictate the design and the required service connections. For example continental-style wet rooms are increasingly popular additions to homes, but these need fairly extensive plumbing connections. There's also a definite trend in people working from home and needing fully equipped office space with a degree of seclusion - so important client calls aren't rudely interrupted by screaming babies and yelping dogs! But in reality the layout of the house may affect the feasibility of plumbing in new kitchens and bathrooms, depending on the position of your existing drains.

Minimising disturbance
Anything that's likely to generate lots of dust, mess and noise, such as sanding, drilling or taking down ceilings, will need very careful planning. Unless you've taken suitable measures to protect and cover furniture and carpets etc, this can cause tempers to fray! The nature of some building works can increase the risk of fire (e.g. paint stripping) so if you haven't got them already, fitting smoke alarms is probably the single most effective survival measure, as well as one of the cheapest.
For major works, make a point of notifying your insurers in writing advance, so they can't wriggle out of a claim should you need to make one.
If you're doing some of the work yourself, be sure to wear protective clothing, goggles, masks, gloves and steel-capped boots, plus a hard hat, where needed. Above all, take extra care when working at height, and ensure that scaffolding is correctly erected.

Budgeting
No matter how carefully you budget for building works there will always be a degree of uncertainty. For example your existing electrics or heating system may need upgrading to cope with the extra demands of supplying an enlarged home. So it's normally a good idea to include a contingency sum

of at least 10%. As we know from TV property shows, it's very easy at this stage to be overly optimistic. So when budgeting, try to be realistic, and don't be tempted to stick down the lowest possible prices.

Labour costs will of course be a major component of the total spend, so if you have the necessary skills to do some of the work yourself it can generate significant savings. When it comes to materials, researching the cost is fairly easy to do online, but don't forget to factor in delivery charges for bulky items, and plan ahead to allow for lead-in times for specialist products such as bespoke glazing, custom-made kitchen units and exotic bathroom suites. Also you need to include any fees for surveyors, structural engineers, and applications for Planning or Building Regulations.

When employing builders, bear in mind that small one-off jobs are proportionately dearer. Unit costs are less if the job is part of larger project where the cost of plant hire and scaffolding can be shared between jobs. Above all, always be clear about what you're actually paying for. Does the price include VAT, scaffolding, carting away all rubbish, and cleaning up afterwards?

Paying for it
There are a number of options when it comes to raising the money to pay for home improvements. Of course the cheapest way of financing any such project is to get someone else to pay for it! And it's not unknown for employers to foot the bill for conversion work to build home-offices for their staff, on the grounds that it's cheaper than paying to rent office space in town. So you could always try putting yours on expenses! But for most of us, more conventional methods of funding will need to be considered:-

* Savings
If you've got a few quid stashed away, the chances are it'll be earning a pittance in miserly interest rates. Using existing savings to fund home improvements is the simplest and cheapest way of financing a project.

* Bank or Building Society loans
Mortgages are normally the least expensive way to borrow money. Lenders know that home improvements are likely to increase your property's value (i.e. their security) and are generally sympathetic to requests for 'further advances' to borrow a bit more on the mortgage. The worst method of funding is with credit cards and unsecured loans as the rates charged can be extortionate.

* Grants & subsidies
From time to time sources of grant funding pop up. But these tend to be targeted at qualifying households, perhaps contingent upon being within a specific age or income group. Local authority grants are sometimes available for provision of special needs facilities, such as bathrooms with disabled access. Even for owners of Listed buildings only in exceptional cases are grants available for urgent repairs (usually via conservation bodies such as English Heritage).

Minimising VAT
There are a number of situations where reduced VAT can apply to residential properties. Perhaps the most obvious exemption is where you employ individuals or small firms with a low annual turnover below the VAT threshold (£85,000 at the time of writing) since they are quite legitimately not required to charge VAT. But your builder will still have to pay VAT on materials and plant hired, and this cost will be passed on to you. Where you are charged VAT, always check the necessary VAT number is shown on the invoice.

Another useful saving can legitimately be made where you are renovating a residential property that has been left empty for at least 2 years since it will be eligible for a reduced VAT rate of 5 per cent. Better still, for properties empty for more than 10 years there is no VAT – i.e. the full amount should be recoverable.

3. Building works and costing the project

There are 5 main ways to get a project built:-

1/ Employ a main contractor (or specialist firm) who does the whole thing for you - designing, building and managing the entire project.

2/ As above, but they only build the 'shell' – you finish it and project manage.

3/ An architect designs and manages it, but a building contractor is employed to build it.

4/ You employ individual trades directly and manage the project (with some optional DIY input).

5/ Do the whole thing yourself – but this is only advisable if you're experienced and have plenty of willing helpers.

DIY projects
Some works are excluded or restricted from the DIY sphere by the Building Regulations, such as any gas fitting and much of the electrics. Otherwise if you're planning to tackle the work yourself it's important to be realistic about how much you can achieve. It's not unusual to encounter something unexpected, and it's very easy to underestimate the time a job will take – so it's not a bad idea to double your first estimate of the likely timescale! And don't forget to budget for your time as a cost (as you could instead have been earning the money to pay a builder).

How much can I do myself ?	
Obviously much will depend on your skills and experience, but the following is a general rule	
Yes **Jobs to consider tackling**	**No** **Best leave it to the professionals**
Decoration and wall tiling	All structural works – new beams, joists to roofs and floors
Fitting the bathroom suite	New dormers and any roofing work
Plumbing	New stairs
Floorboarding and floor coverings	Electrics

Plasterboarding & dry lining	Plastering
Insulating	Compliance with Fire Regs
Internal partition walls	
Door hanging	
Fitting windows	
Project management	

Finding the right people for the job
Unless you are doing the work yourself, you will need to find the right builder and agree a price.

*Choosing a builder
The success of any building project is to a large extent down to your choice of builders. But anyone with a van can offer building services, so it's essential to do your homework. Architects and surveyors can be a useful source of advice as they may have worked with contractors and key trades on previous jobs. However local recommendations are often best - perhaps your friends or neighbours can suggest a good builder - but you still need to check them out.
You also need to decide whether to appoint a main contractor or to directly employ individual trades. Either way, it's important that they come with good references. Inevitably however the best people tend to be booked up weeks or months in advance.

* Quotes & estimates

A *quote* is a firm price that is legally binding - a fixed sum for a fixed amount of work. Unless you request extras or agreed to any changes this is the amount you should end up paying. An *estimate,* on the other hand, is nothing more than the builder's best guess as to what the cost might eventually be.

For smaller, straightforward jobs a brief, clearly written description and a scale drawing may be all that's required for a builder to quote against.

Where you're employing individual trades, the best arrangement is to confirm acceptance of their written quote in writing. For smaller jobs, a simple exchange of letters and copies of any approved plans is often sufficient. The letter should include all the key points such as the agreed price, the payment terms and the start & finish dates. For larger projects it's a good idea to type out a specification, which is basically a long 'shopping list' stating each separate piece of work you want done against which the contractor has to price.

To select a contractor for a major project it's advisable to send out tenders to about 4 or 5 local firms including a copy of the Building Control approved drawings and a suitable contract (such as the free Federation of Master Builders contract (available from www.period-house.com). All you need to do is to fill in the key details, such as the agreed price, the start & completion dates, and payment terms. Then both parties sign and keep a copy.

* Professional advice

In more complex cases professional advice may be needed - but avoid 'free' advice from specialist contractors with a vested interest to drum up work.

A Building Surveyor or Architect can be appointed to draw up plans, write a specification and obtain quotes or tender the job. For larger projects they should be able to perform the role of project manager and administer the contract.

To find the right people, start by checking out the relevant professional bodies, or visit a website such as www.rightsurvey.co.uk with links to all the main professions. Qualified architects are members of RIBA and Chartered Surveyors are members of RICS. To design structural alterations you normally need to appoint a Structural Engineer with professional qualifications such as MICE or MIStructE. Above all, pick someone you feel comfortable working with and check they have professional indemnity insurance in place.

Managing the project

The key to a successful outcome is to specify clearly at the outset precisely what you want done, and ensure this is clearly communicated to the people doing the job. It also pays to build some slack into your programme, whilst keeping the builders focussed on completion by the agreed date.

Carefully managing your finances is also of prime importance. No one does their best work if they're not paid on time. But never pay for work in advance – in case the builder goes bust or vanishes without trace!

On larger projects where you're paying in stages for completed work, it's a good idea to agree with the contractor to keep a small retention (say 5% of the total cost of each payment). The retention is only released after the end of the project when your 'snagging list' of all the minor outstanding bits has been completed.

When the project is nearly finished it's important to notify Building Control to carry out their final site inspection and request the Completion Certificate. Despite the name, this can be done soon after 2nd fix stage, prior to decoration and minor finishing works. So you will still need to chase the builders later to ensure things like snagging and decoration are fully completed.

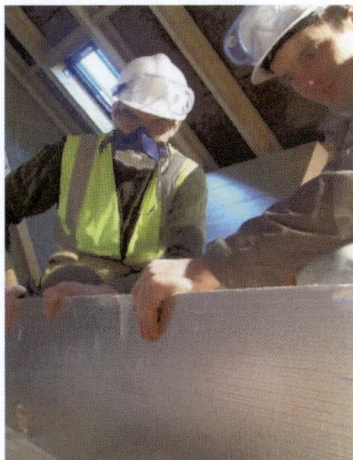

- Get at least 3 written quotes (not estimates). For larger jobs this should be priced against an itemised specification that you've provided. Get the cost broken down into as much detail as possible, so you can see what you're getting and use it as a guide for any additional works.

- When comparing quotes, check for hidden extras, and don't be tempted to automatically choose the lowest price

- Check if VAT is included in the quote. Individual trades my have a turnover that's below the VAT threshold and quite legitimately not need to charge.

- Ask for references from previous jobs, and go and see them

- Never pay up front. Agree payment stages in advance and only pay for completed work.

- Check that the builder is insured for risks to persons and property. Ask for copies of certificates for full public liability insurance and (for main contractors) employers' liability cover.

- Be very clear about precisely what work you want done and once you've accepted a quote don't keep changing your mind or you will be charged lots of expensive extras.

- Use a written contract with firms or detailed letters with trades

- Confirm the start and finish dates in writing, along with the agreed price and arrangements for payment.

- Confirm exactly what's included in the price – e.g. does it include lifting and re-laying carpets, moving furniture, scaffolding, clearing rubbish, skip hire and cleaning up?

4. Getting consent - Planning & Building Regs

In Part 2 we look in detail at 8 major projects and in each case explain whether Planning or Building Regulations applies. In most cases planning consent isn't required, because much conversion and extending work is classed as 'Permitted Development'. But in some cases these rights won't apply, for example where they're prevented by a condition in the original planning permission for the house. And if you happen to live in a Conservation Area, or the building you're working on is Listed, consent may well be needed. And when it comes to complying with the Building Regulations in most cases you will need to make an application to Building Control.

* Making a Building Regs application
One of the most important things with any development is ensuring that the design fully complies with the Building Regulations. These are technical standards published in the form of 'Approved Documents' which you can download free online. The Building Regulations apply in more areas than you might imagine. The key 'Approved Documents' are:-

A   Structure
B   Fire safety
C   Site preparation
D   Toxic substances
E   Resistance to the passage of sound
F   Ventilation and condensation
G   Hygiene, hot water safety and water efficiency
H   Drainage & waste disposal
J   Combustion appliances & fuel storage systems
K   Stairs, ramps, guards and glazing (formerly Part N)
L   Conservation of fuel and power
M   Access to and use of buildings
P   Electrical safety

There are 2 ways of making an application - a 'proper' Full Plans application, or the short-cut method known as a Building Notice. The fee is the same in both cases.

* Full Plans Application

With this method, you or your designer will need to submit drawings of the proposed work together with supporting information, a completed application form and the appropriate fee. Unlike simpler planning drawings, these need to include detailed information confirming compliance, such as specifying precise details of openings and the strengths and thermal performance of materials. You may also need to provide engineer's calculations for structural work as part of your application.

Following any necessary clarification a 'plans approval' letter is normally issued. Work can start any time after the application has been received although it's normally advisable to wait 2 to 3 weeks until the key details have been checked. You (or your builder) will need to notify Building Control at least 2 days prior to start on site. The work is then inspected at key stages as it progresses on site. The application itself should take no more than 5 weeks. As with planning consent, once approval has been granted you need to use it or lose it, and start work within a 3 year period.

* Building Notice Application

With this method you are basically making a promise up front that you will comply with the Building Regulations on site, rather than submitting detailed drawings to prove it in advance. However further information is sometimes required, such as structural calculations or drawings. Work can commence 48 hours after the notice has been accepted. The risk with this method is that a site inspection could later uncover something that doesn't comply. And if a problem isn't picked up until late in the day, it could involve considerable extra work for it to be taken down and rebuilt. So it is best suited for very small projects carried out by a competent builder. Here, no formal approval of plans is issued and instead work is approved on site as it progresses.

Self Certification

Approval of works such as electrical wiring, replacement windows, heating installations is normally delegated via approved installers registered as 'competent persons' who can certify that work has been carried out in compliance with the Building Regs. Certain trade bodies are allowed to 'self-certify' their members' work and issue completion certificates:-

* FENSA – Contractors registered with Fenestration Self Assessment (FENSA) can self-certify the compliance of their replacement window works (not required where only the glass is being replaced).

* CERTASS – Contractors registered with CERTASS (which stands for 'Certification and Assessment') can also self-certify that their replacement window installations adhere to current Building Regulations– as an alternative to FENSA.

* GAS SAFE – Gas Safe registered contractors can issue certificates for installations and alterations to gas, hot water and heating systems. But the contractor must be a registered member, not just a service engineer.

* OFTEC – the equivalent of Gas Safe for oil fired boilers and appliances

* HETAS – the equivalent of Gas Safe for solid fuel burning boilers and appliances

* Electrical Contractors – must be registered under one of the 'Part P' schemes in order to issue certificates for domestic electrical work.

Tips for using Self Certified Contractors

1. Ensure the contractor is registered for the specific type of work they're undertaking.

2. At the end of the job make sure they issue you with a completion certificate – before settling the bill in full. This confirms the work complies with the Building Regulations.

3. If there's any doubt about the contractor's registration and membership get in touch with their trade association, or contact Building Control before confirming their appointment.

You can check whether a contractor holds the appropriate degree of competency by visiting the 'competent persons register' www.competentperson.co.uk

Making a Planning Application
Where a planning application needs to be made, it's always worth getting in touch with the Planners to talk through your proposals in advance. In most cases it's also worth discussing your plans with an architect or surveyor. Then you will need to submit the completed application forms together with the necessary drawings and an appropriate fee to the Development Control Department at the local authority. Once your application has been accepted, you normally need to allow a period of 8 weeks for it to be processed and, hopefully, recommended for approval.

It's not unknown for people to take a mad gamble by building or converting illegally without planning consent in the hope that immunity from enforcement action can be acquired after a period of time has elapsed. This rule is 4 years for the development or use of a building (or part of a building) as a dwelling house. But a period of 10 years applies where planning conditions are breached. However, the 'second bite' rule can sometimes allow Councils to take further enforcement action outside the usual time limits.

The Party Wall Act
If you need to carry out building work to a wall shared your neighbours, the Part Wall Act comes into play. This is a legal requirement that is totally separate from Planning and Building Control.
As well as affecting party walls between adjoining terraced and semi detached houses, it can also apply where you want to excavate foundations within 3m of an adjoining property (in some cases within 6m), and can also apply to boundary walls between gardens. This normally means having to appoint a Party Wall Surveyor. Further info can be obtained at www.planningportal.gov.uk

PART 2
8 ways of making more space

* Loft Conversions

* Extensions

* Conservatories

* Garage conversions

* Outbuilding conversions

* Garden buildings

* Opening up useable space

* Basement conversions

1.
Converting Your Loft

Think how much more useful your loft would be as a bedroom, a home-office or a playroom rather than a dusty refuge for Xmas decorations and boxes of assorted junk. And when it comes to adding value, loft conversions are regularly voted to be the optimum home improvement. Better still, the work can often be done at relatively low cost. One reason for this is that foundations and roofs - the big-ticket costs – are already in place.

Loft conversions cost about a third the price of digging out a basement, and are significantly cheaper than building extensions - plus they don't consume precious garden space.

But some properties are cheaper to convert than others. A house with a reasonably spacious loft and an existing entrance hall (to comply with Fire Regs) is a good start. And if your design only needs a couple of skylights fitted, they will typically costs around 70% less to install than constructing dormer windows.

Questions to ask up front

Before your conversion to loft-living can start in earnest some key points need to be checked:-

* Is your house suitable?
Not all properties can be easily converted. Fairly obviously, the loft space needs to be large enough to provide a useable room. Ideally the overall footprint of the loft floor should be at least 5 x 5 metres although narrower lofts can sometimes be made wider by adding a large box dormer. But the critical factor is of course headroom. If you can stand up in the loft and raise your arm without obstruction, there's a good chance that it's ripe for conversion. You'd normally want to see at least 2.6 metres clear headroom at the apex, bearing in mind that the new floor in a converted loft will be around 200mm higher than the old ceiling joists. Disappointment is more likely in 1970s properties with their shallow pitched roofs, although there are ways this can sometimes be solved - see ''Problem Solving' below.

* What's it for?
How would you use the extra space? A bedroom with an en-suite bathroom is the most popular arrangement, but loft rooms sometimes have limitations - for example toddlers and some oldies may struggle with steep loft stairs. And for obvious reasons items like pianos and gym equipment are better suited to ground floors. If you want an en-suite in your new loft accommodation then the best place to locate it is above an existing bathroom, so both waste and hot and cold supply pipes can connect without major expense and hassle. Extractor fans will also be required to new bathrooms.

* What kind of roof have I got?
As well as noting how generous the headroom is in your loft, another key point to check the side of your roof (unless it's a mid terrace). Normally this will either comprise a triangular gable wall or a sloping hipped roof common in 1930s properties. A hipped side roof can sometimes pose problems where it coincides with the position of your new loft stairs and may need to be raised, either by adding a side dormer or by converting the hip to a gable.

In terms of the roof structure, the easiest type to convert is the traditional 'cut timber' roof found in most pre-1950s properties. These were custom-built on site with timber rafters forming the skeleton of each roof slope, normally supported by a long, chunky, timber purlin running underneath. After the war timber was in short supply, so an economical new structure was developed – the manufactured roof truss. Early 'TDA' trussed roofs still had traditional rafters and purlins but these were supported with 3 or 4 trusses, typically comprising twin strips of 'A' shaped timber bolted together.

By the late 1960s these were in turn superseded by modern prefabricated 'fink trusses', with their distinctive 'W' shaped webbing. Here each triangular set of rafters, ceiling joists and webbing is manufactured as one giant flat component ready to be craned into place one by one to form the roof structure. The resulting forests of thin timber webbing obstructing modern lofts can at first be rather off-putting. But although once regarded as 'hard to convert' on account of their relatively slender roof timbers (typically only about 30 x 70mm), many lofts of this type have been successfully transformed into useable living space. The key is to 'preserve the triangulation' ensuring that the opposing roof slopes are fully supported and tied together at the base (e.g. with new floor joists) and near the apex with new collars. Also, it's essential that the new structure is fully in place before cutting any of the trusses. The rafters may also need to be strengthened by doubling them up with new ones fixed alongside, or lined internally with sheets of OSB which should also improve the rigidity of the structure and provide windbracing.

Planning and Building Regulations

Planning applications

As long as you don't raise the height of your roof or change your home's external appearance, in most cases you won't need planning consent as the 'Permitted Development Rules' should apply. Whereas fitting skylights doesn't normally require permission, building a new dormer will - because it alters the roof line. But even big, bulky dormers are generally acceptable when tucked away out of sight on rear elevations, although this can depend on any concerns about 'overlooking'. However, large side dormers or 'hip to gable' conversions are more contentious, and may need approval.

In terms of additional space, the rules are surprisingly generous. Conversions are permitted that don't exceed 50 cubic metres (40 cu m. for terraced properties) subject to a maximum increase of 20% of the overall volume of the property. This is the extra amount you can build *in addition to* your existing loft space, so unless your dormers are the size of a Zeppelin it should be OK. Of course if you live in a Listed building or in a Conservation Area, or want to build higher than the original roof, planning permission will be required.

Complying with Building Regs

All loft conversions need Building Regulations consent. Although primarily this is concerned with matters of safety (structural support, safe access, escape from fire etc), complying with 'Part L' to meet thermal efficiency U-value targets is becoming increasingly important. Consent is also required for works to the electrics, glazing and roof coverings but these can normally be self-certified by approved installers. Fortunately, when it comes to loft stairs, Part K of the Building Regulations adopts a pragmatic approach – see 'where do I put the stairs' below.
Once your application has been approved by Local Authority Building Control, the building works will then be inspected at key stages. Building Control Officers are a good source of technical advice for matters such as complying with fire regulations and provision of loft stairs.

A number of different regulations apply to most loft conversions including Part A (structure), B (fire), F (ventilation), K (stairs), L (energy conservation) and P (electrics), and in some cases E (sound), H (drainage) as well. Although this may sound daunting, don't be tempted to convert without consent. Apart from the risk of fines and enforced demolition, a dodgy loft will cause problems when you come to sell. If there's no completion certificate to prove the works have been checked and legally comply, buyers may walk away. So before making the final payment to the contractor, be sure to obtain your completion certificate from Building Control and keep a small retention to cover any minor snagging works.

Designing your new space

A decent-sized loft may only require a couple of discreet skylights fitted flush with the roof slopes. In most cases however, the amount of living space will largely depend on how big a dormer window the planners will accept. But giant flat-roofed dormers can look overbearing externally, which is why they are normally banished to the rear of the property. The choice is essentially between 'large box' and 'full width' dormers. As the name suggests, the former are basically big boxes poking out of the roof with some original tiling left in place around them. Full-width dormers are even wider, with their side 'cheeks' built up from the property's existing side (or party) walls. 'Mansards' are a variation on this theme with their front walls leaning back to form a very steep roof slope, with a flat or shallow main roof above. Mansards are a useful device for minimising visual bulk and are widely applied to Georgian and Victorian townhouses.

Another tool in the designer's box is the traditional small 'cottage dormer'. These can improve the look of even the plainest dwellings, but unfortunately don't provide much extra space inside. There is a wide range of materials to choose from when it comes to cladding your dormer walls – timber boarding, lead sheeting, render, UPVC, tile or slate. Pitched dormer roofs are normally clad in tile or slate to match the main roof, but flat roofs are best finished in good quality lead since a cheap flat felted finish can become a maintenance headache within 10 to15 years.

Designing the structure

For most conversions the new structural work involves inserting a pair of steel beams across the ceiling joists in the loft, typically set about a metre in from the front and rear, and bedded into the main side walls. These will provide support for beefy new floor joists run alongside the old thin ceiling joists. In some designs, a timber stud 'purlin wall' can be built on top of the beams to support the main roof rafters higher up at purlin level (without the need for another pair of steel beams under the rafters). If you're adding a large dormer window, a single steel beam under the ridge of the main roof will support the new joists for the flat roof.

Altering period properties

If you live in a charming period property (i.e. pre 1930s) adding new loadings to crumbling old walls might not be such a brilliant idea. Older properties with shallow foundations can sometimes struggle to accommodate major additional loads. Party walls may only be made of single width brick (115mm thick) and not up to the job of supporting new steel beams. And ancient timber lintels over window and door openings may have been weakened by beetle or fungal decay. One solution might be to use special telescopic beams which have the advantage of spreading loadings over a wider area than steels with their very high point loadings.

However older buildings usually have internal load-bearing 'spine walls' of solid masonry construction. It may be possible to utilise this intermediate support for new floor joists running from one main wall to the other, obviating the need for new steel beams. However, to be certain that internal walls are sufficiently robust to cope with extra loadings it's advisable to appoint a structural engineer to check foundation depths (and to provide the necessary calculations to support your Building Control application).

The 'nuclear option' would be to erect a totally independent supporting framework to support the new beams at roof level, with steel stanchions erected on concrete pad foundations excavated in your ground floor rooms. However this could add more than £10,000 plus enormous upheaval, and in most cases simply wouldn't be cost-effective.

What's it going to cost?

The average loft conversion costs between about £15,000 and £40,000 depending on the design and how hard the house is to convert. When budgeting it's best to set aside at least a further 10% to cover unforeseen expenditure, such as upgrading your home's heating and electrics to cope with the extra demand.

Approximate costs for a typical loft conversion	
(actual costs will depend on design, house type, and market labour rates)	
	£
Design drawings including engineer's calculations	2000
Fees for planning & building regs	1300
Structural work to floor and roof	12000
2 new roof windows	2000
New large box dormer	4000
Insulation	3500
Electrics and plumbing	2800

En suite bathroom	2500
Stairs & stud walls	3000
Fire doors	2000
Dry lining & skim plastering	3500
Decoration, tiling and finishing	2500

N.B. excludes any necessary additional work to open-plan properties to comply with Fire Regs

Talk to your neighbours
Unless you live in a detached house, the works will almost certainly affect the party wall that divides you from next door. So by law you must comply with the Party Wall Act. This is something contractors sometimes conveniently forget. It means having to formally notify your neighbours at least 2 months in advance of any works. Unless they agree, you may have to appoint a surveyor to draw up an agreement before work can start.

Where do I put the stairs?
The new loft stairs can often be run directly above the existing staircase, a common solution in Victorian houses. In some 1930s to 1960s properties you may be able to utilise the generous cupboard space between the front and rear main bedrooms, so the new stairs can run sideways off the landing toward the party wall. Otherwise part of a bedroom may need to be partitioned off.

Where space is very tight, the good news is the Building Regs rules for loft stairs are surprisingly relaxed. Instead of the normal requirement for 2 metres of headroom above each stair tread, it is recognised that ceilings to loft stairs may need to slope (e.g. under hipped roofs). So a reduced space of 1.9m above the centre line of the stairs and 1.8m on the lower side can be acceptable as long as you can achieve 2m on the higher side. Although a minimum tread width of only 600mm should be acceptable in most cases, if space is really cramped special space-saver stairs may be permitted - either alternating tread 'paddle stairs' or 'fixed ladder' stairs with handrails both sides, or even spiral stairs. This may be acceptable where the new accommodation comprises just a single habitable room.

The position of new steels can sometimes clash with stairs, so the alternative of using telescopic joists may be worth considering (see below). Note also that the stairs should be provided with a handrail at least 900mm high, and any open sides should be protected with balustrading to the same height, to prevent falling.

Fire!
At the heart of any design for converting a loft there must be an acceptable method of escape, so the occupants won't get burned to a frazzle in the event of fire. Since the rules changed in 2007 it has no longer been acceptable to rely solely on a 'means of escape window' that can be accessed in an emergency from outside. So the primary method of escape is normally via an 'escape corridor' leading down from your loft room to a 'final exit door' (e.g. the front door). This is easy to achieve in properties with a traditional entrance hall. Here the existing walls and ceilings enclosing the hall, stairs and landing should already provide the necessary 30 minutes resistance, doubling as an escape corridor without the need for lining with extra layers of fireboard. However where the sides or underside of staircases are accessible from the kitchen or a reception room, a protective lining of fireboard with a skim plaster finish will be required.
Compliance is more challenging in homes with open plan layouts, which may need a new partition wall to be built creating a fire-resistant hallway, sacrificing valuable living space.

 To contain the smoke and flames long enough for you to escape, doors to all habitable rooms en-route as well as to the new loft accommodation itself must provide minimum 20 minutes fire-resistance. However they not required to bathrooms, WCs and utility rooms, and fitting self-closers to doors is no longer required. This normally means having to replace most of your existing internal doors with new fire doors (rated FD20 or higher) – a requirement that builders are sometimes tempted to overlook. However, if you have valuable antique doors, it should be possible to retain them by instead upgrading with special fire-resistant paint or fire-seals.

There are possible alternative solutions, such as constructing a new lobby at the base of an enclosed fire-boarded staircase with a choice of escape routes via 2 fire-doors, leading to separate main exits. Building Control can exercise discretion and in some cases may accept interlinked smoke alarms installed in all rooms with no need for fire doors. Inevitably, compliance is more arduous with taller multi-storey buildings where the new floor is more than 7.5m above external ground level and in some cases provision of an external fire escape or sprinkler systems may be required, significantly adding to the expense.

Keeping it warm

The second most common complaint about new lofts is that, like conservatories, they sometimes overheat (the most common complaint being a lack of headroom!). But applying the correct insulation to retain warmth in winter and to stay cool in summer is now a major part of the job. A common solution is to fit 70mm thick polyurethane insulation boards between the rafters, having first left a 50mm space under the tiles for ventilation. Then a further 50mm layer of insulation is applied to the room-side of the rafters. To comply with energy conservation requirements in 'Part L' of the Building Regs all wall and ceiling surfaces must be fully insulated.

Lighting

It is claimed that roof windows allow an amazing 8 times as much light into a room compared to the equivalent wall window. Facing the sky certainly helps boost the light, so a couple of fairly small skylights may be all you need. This arrangement also minimises heat loss from windows. Light tubes or flat roof domes are also worth considering, and small gable end windows can sometimes work wonders.

Tricky bits

Tanks and old stored stuff

The need for large water tanks in lofts in lofts is rapidly becoming a thing of the past, with the advent of mains fed combination boilers or pressurised unvented hot water systems. Where water tanks need to be re-instated they can be placed within new eaves cupboards occupying the low-ceilinged 'dead space' around the edges of the room. Eaves cupboards (or a new mini-loft under the apex) can also come in useful for storing any remaining stuff from the old loft that couldn't be chucked out or sold.

Ventilation

When fitting insulation to the rafters, the Building Regulations require a clear air space of 50mm to be left between the rafters under the tiles. A good flow of air is required from the eaves on one side to the opposite side of the building to safely disperse any moist air. In some cases additional vents may be required to eaves and ridge tiles. There are no special requirements for room ventilation, just conventional trickle vents on openable windows, plus extractor fans in bathrooms.

Soundproofing

The walls and floors around new bedrooms will need to be insulated to reduce sound transmission. One of the best materials for this purpose is mineral wool (in quilt or batt form), which can be stuffed between floor joists or timber studwork. Lining walls and ceilings with a double layer of acoustic plasterboard can also be very effective (as can laying a carpet over thick rubber underlay). For best results consider laying acoustic floor boards to the loft room and constructing a suspended ceiling to the rooms below stuffed with mineral wool.

If you are converting a loft in a terraced or semi-detached house you will also need to upgrade the sound resistance of the party wall.

Employing builders and comparing quotes

There are many specialist loft conversion firms who can do a 'package deal' covering just about everything – at a price. But you still need to compare quotes carefully. Check what's not included, such as - tiling and decoration, floor coverings, supplying bathroom fittings, structural engineers' fees, and planning & building control applications. To help compare like-with-like download a free quote comparison checklist at www.loft-rooms.com

But package deals tend to be relatively expensive, so to save money you could get specialists in to do the structural work, but source builders or individual trades for the rest. But don't just pick any builder from Yellow Pages. Try to source experienced contractors via recommendations, check their previous loft projects and get at least three quotes.

Employing non-English-speaking trades can cause communication problems. A roofer who has just arrived from say Bulgaria will have a different way of working that doesn't take account of UK Building Regs. Apart from a designer, the only professionals you need to employ are a structural engineer at the design stage, and possibly a surveyor for any party wall issues.

Minimising disturbance
A basic conversion should take 6 to 10 weeks and the order of works should be programmed to minimise inconvenience to the occupants. To save traipsing muck and mess through your house, access to the loft should be via the scaffolding and a new roof window opening. This allows you to postpone fitting the loft stairs and the upheaval of 'breaking through' until as late as possible.

Problem Solving

There are a surprising number of properties with 'the wrong sort of loft' for conversion. Probably most challenging of all are buildings with shallow pitched roofs – and chronically restricted interior headroom. There are a number of possible ways around these sorts of the problems, although it will obviously cost more to do the job.

Removal and rebuild

Where the vertical space inside a roof is in short supply, the obvious solution is to remove the existing roof structure and replace it with a larger one. 'Room-in-roof' trusses can be craned into place to form the shell of a ready-made new loft room, with the insulation placed above the rafters for maximum thermal efficiency. The main problem with 'raising the roof' is that it requires planning consent and there's a fairly good chance this will be refused, especially for terraced or semi-detached homes. But 'removal and rebuild' can take well over a month to complete, and living in a house with no roof is not much fun in a cold, rainy climate, even when the site is cocooned under a temporary canopy. So it can make sense to go one better and pre-fabricate the entire replacement roof in advance. Modular replacement systems can be installed and watertight in 2 days, and because most of the work is factory engineered in advance (including the electrics, plumbing, windows and doors) the whole job can be completed in a fortnight, although roof tiling is normally done on site. Ready-made loft rooms typically work out from around £1,000 per m2 floor area, costing upwards of £60,000, although economies of scale make this a more cost effective solution for larger lofts.

Borrowing space from the rooms below

Instead of going to all the expense and trouble of raising the height of the roof, a less drastic solution involves borrowing 'spare' headroom from the rooms below. In many older properties upstairs ceiling heights are surprisingly generous, and can easily accommodate a loss of space and still leave ample headroom of at least 2.2 metres. This method differs from conventional loft conversions where the existing ceiling joists are retained and new floor joists (typically 200mm deep) run alongside, supported on steel beams inserted at right angles above ceiling level.

To capitalise on the unused space down below the new joists can instead be fitted below the existing ceiling level, with additional support from 'long legged' joist hangers extended beneath the steels. Once the new floor is in place the old ceiling can be cut away, freeing up at least 200mm of space. The extra work involved should add no more than about 10% to the total cost.

Telescopic beams and restricted space

Most loft conversions employ at least one pair of steel beams to support the new floor structure and the roof slopes at purlin level, and sometimes also at ridge level, e.g. where you're adding a large dormer. However, manoeuvring long, heavy steels into place at high level can be enormously difficult, necessitating the use of shorter 2m lengths bolted together in situ. Even then, it's pretty hefty work because steel beams can weigh as much as 100kg per metre!

Where access is restricted, '*TeleBeams*' can provide an ingenious solution. These are extendable lightweight aluminium beams that are slid into place alongside the existing floor joists. Costs are reduced because you only need to remove the lower 3 rows of tiles on one side of the house, so there's no need to hire a crane to install heavy steel beams. Being telescopic, the beams can be adjusted to the width of the building, spanning from outside wall to outside wall. As well as forming the new floor structure, they also provide support to the roof rafters via vertical stud walls near the edges of the room. This will often work out cheaper than using conventional steels once you factor in savings on labour, access and plant hire etc. The system has 'National Type Approval' so structural calculations don't need to be submitted for Building Regulations, but you may still need a steel beam at ridge level where you have a large dormer.

2.
Building An Extension

Adding a new extension to your home is the probably the most obvious way of making more space. Unlike loft conversions, extensions are ideal for creating large kitchen/diners or reception rooms. In fact the new accommodation can suit just about all uses, including bedrooms and bathrooms to upper floors. But extensions have a reputation for being expensive to build – hence the enduring appeal of conservatories. But the fact is, if you keep it simple, it needn't cost a fortune. An extension basically comprises 3 walls and a roof. So we're going to see how you can get a great extension built on a budget.

QUESTIONS TO ASK UP FRONT
Before starting some key points need to be checked:-

* Can you extend without planning permission? Often the answer is 'yes' – see Permitted Development Rights below. However you will still need to make a Building Regulations application.

* Is my house suitable? Some properties are easier (and cheaper) to extend than others; it helps if you've got a clear run without having to divert things like boilers and drainage pipes

* What will it cost? You won't know for sure without getting quotes but there are lots of ways to keep the price down – see 'doing it on a budget' below.

Minimising disturbance

You don't want your home to be overwhelmed by the building works. So it's important to arrange things so that life can carry on as normal.

* Access for labour and materials can cause enormous disruption. You don't want muddy boots and wheelbarrows endlessly traipsing through your hallway. This can be tricky in terraced houses where there's no side gate to the garden, but there are ways this can be resolved – see 'Access Issues' below.

* Deliveries: So that building materials can be delivered and safely stored it's a good idea to allocate space in advance – or they'll probably just get plonked down by your front door.

* Constant dust and noise can drive you potty. So leave the 'knocking through' until as late as possible, keeping separating walls in place as a protective barrier as long as possible. Then be sure to cover furniture etc with dust sheets when the extension is opened up to the house. You might also want to agree some things in advance with the builders such as the time work starts on site each day.

* Services: The existing electrics, plumbing & heating systems normally need to be extended. But leave this as late as possible, then schedule a day for the work when the main supplies can be temporarily cut off without causing too much disruption.

* Loo breaks: to save builders sprinkling on your pristine porcelain day-in, day-out, you might want to hire a handy port-a-loo. Or plant a handy hedge!

PLANNING APPLICATIONS

In many cases extensions can be built quite legitimately without the need for planning permission.

Permitted Development Rights (PDRs)

'Permitted Development Rights' are a 'free allowance' that allow you to build out without the need for a planning application. These are the basic rules:-

Front

No extension allowed in front of your '**principal elevation'** - normally the front main wall.
However small porches are permitted if :

* Under 3 sq metres floor area
* Maximum 3 metres high
* Set back at least 2 metres from roads or footpaths

Side

Extensions are permitted to the side as long as they are single storey, subject to :-

*Maximum height : 4 metres
*Maximum width: up to half width of original house

N.B. if the side of your house counts as the 'principle elevation', e.g. where your side wall faces a highway - then no extension is allowed

Rear

Quite large extensions are permitted to the rear, both single and multiple storey. The size rules were increased from 2013 doubling the previous limits. So you can now build up to 8 metres deep for single storey rear extensions to detached houses, and up to 6 metres deep for terraced and semi-detached houses, or for extensions of more than a single storey to detached houses. Previously the limit was 4m and 3m respectively. The maximum height for single storey extensions remains at 4 metres. However, a homeowner wishing to build an extension greater than the previous Permitted Development limits will first need to write to the local planning authority to apply for 'prior approval', submitting plans and a description of the proposal. The local authority will then notify adjoining neighbours who will have 21 days to make an objection. If no objection is received the homeowner will be able to proceed.

If any neighbour raises an objection, the local authority will then consider whether the impact of the proposed extension on the amenity of the neighbours is acceptable.

Subject to…

If the above allowances sound too good to be true, bear in mind that some additional rules apply that may restrict what you can build:-

Height

Extensions must be no higher than the highest part of the main roof
The eaves and ridge height must also be no higher than those of existing house
For extensions within 2 metres of a boundary, the maximum eaves height is limited to 3 metres.
And higher extensions of 2 storeys or more must be no closer than 7 metres to your rear garden boundary

Garden plot

You're allowed to cover up to half the land around the 'original house' with buildings. This includes any previous extensions which must be taken into account (unless you demolish them). Once this limit has been used up you need planning permission.

Conservation Areas & Listed

The rules are less generous for properties located in Conservation Areas. Here, no extensions are permitted to the front or side of the building, and to the rear they must only be single storey. But it could be worse – for Listed buildings nothing is permitted!

Planning conditions

When planning consent is granted for the development of new homes, it's not unusual for a condition to be included that removes Permitted Development Rights. So if your property was built fairly recently, this should be checked. In fact it's worth checking with the Planners anyway because PDRs are occasionally removed for other reasons (e.g. 'article 4 directions').

Planning principles

Where a planning application needs to be made, it's always worth getting in touch with the Planners to talk through your proposals in advance. It's also worth considering some of the ways that designs are likely to be judged, so you don't waste time drawing up detailed plans for something they're going to consider to be a definite no-hoper. There are usually ways of compromising and finding common ground to make an application acceptable.

In most cases it's also worth discussing your plans with an architect or surveyor. Then you will need to submit the completed application forms together with the necessary drawings and an appropriate fee to the Development Control Department at the local authority. Once your application has been accepted, you normally need to allow a period of 8 weeks for it to be processed and, hopefully, recommended for approval. If it's unreasonably rejected you have a right of appeal, but it's much better to get it right first time around.

*Overlooking

No one wants nosy neighbours staring down at them from an observation tower they've stuck on the back of their house. This is why 'overlooking' can be the death knell for designs featuring prominent balconies or first floor conservatories. In fairness, a certain amount of 'overlooking' can be hard to avoid from windows. Where this is an issue, there are a number of possible solutions, such as offering to fit obscure frosted glass, or you could maybe substitute standard windows for skylights at roof level that face harmlessly upwards. Locating windows higher up (so they're above eye level) is usually acceptable, with a sill height at least 1.7 metres above internal floor level. Or in some cases overlooking can be reduced by erecting screen walls or fences in the garden.

*The 45 degree guideline

There are limits on how far you're reasonably allowed to build out from the back of the house into the garden. The question is, will your extension 'overshadow' the neighbours, or blot out their sunshine? Find out by taking a plan drawing of the proposed extension and sketching an imaginary 45 degree line from the outermost corner of the new extension back towards next door's house. This casts an imaginary shadow over the adjoining property. The rule is, the 'shadow' mustn't cover their window closest to you (habitable rooms only – so it's utility rooms and cloakrooms don't count).

*Parking

Making your house larger by adding extra rooms can potentially mean more car-owning occupants – even if this population boom would only materialise in the distant future after you've sold the house. So the Planners may want you to provide new off-street parking to compensate for any loss of garages or car spaces. They will also want to consult the Highways Department about any new driveways, and will also seek their opinion as to whether your proposed extension would interfere with visibility for motorists.

Side extensions should be set back from the main building line

*Set backs
Side extensions often need to be 'set-back' slightly (perhaps 100 -150mm) from the main house. This makes extensions look less bulky and can disguise tricky joints.

THE BUILDING REGULATIONS

Compliance with the Building Regulations applies in more areas than you might imagine. In addition to key aspects such as structural integrity, fire safety and drainage, your design will need to demonstrate in some detail how the levels of insulation comply with Part L - conservation of fuel and power.

However approval of works such as electrical wiring, window installation, and heating systems are normally delegated via approved installers registered as *'competent persons'* who can certify that work has been carried out in full compliance.

The best advice is to submit a 'full plans' application in advance to Building Control so they can confirm the design meets all the required standards before work starts. It will also mean you will have an approved set of plans to work to on site. Drawings normally need to be accompanied by engineer's calculations and must include detailed information, specifying precise details of openings and the strengths and thermal performance of materials. At the end of the job a completion certificate should be obtained from Building Control, as this provides important confirmation of compliance when you come to sell.

Exemptions

Some new buildings are exempt from compliance with the Building Regs, for example:-

Porches are exempt where:-
* Maximum 3 m2 floor area
* Glazing is safety glass
* Separated from dwelling by external quality doors / windows

New detached garages are exempt where:-
* Max 30 m2 floor area
* Sited more than 1 metre from any boundary, or built from non-combustible materials

WHAT'S IT GOING TO COST?

There are a number of potential 'hidden costs' that tend to get overlooked when building extensions. If you don't plan for these in advance the builders will charge an arm and a leg to sort them later on site. So remember to budget for things like the possible need to reposition boilers with awkwardly sited flues, to divert downpipes, and build over drain runs – see 'problem solving' below.

Doing it on a budget

There are 5 golden rules for keeping costs as low as possible:-

i. Keep the design simple – see below.

ii. Do the non-structural work yourself.

iii. Project manage and employ trades direct.

iv. Leave kitchen or bathroom fittings until later when funds permit.

v. Write a shopping list of materials and submit to several suppliers for competitive quotes, then negotiate the best price. It helps if the materials are 'off the shelf' either from DIY Stores or builders merchants, or via online suppliers. eBay can be a good source of discounted fittings.

Keep it simple

To keep costs down try to design it along the following lines:-

* Single storey, square or rectangular in plan

* Walls of conventional cavity masonry wall construction (e.g. rendered blockwork)

* Standard trench foundations (avoiding underground obstacles such as drains)

* Simple flat roof

* One room / open-plan internally

* Standard sized door and window openings

* DIY- friendly and designed for 'off-the-shelf' materials

* Design it as a reception room: kitchens and bathrooms add to the cost, and need plumbing in

Employing builders

To get accurate quotes for building work you need to be very clear about what you want. So write down a list of specific works which you can use to get quotes, together with a set of drawings. There are free downloads of sample specifications on the website www.home-extension.co.uk

Try to get at least 3 quotes for any large works. Once you've got them you need to compare them carefully. Check what's not included, such as – clearing away waste, scaffolding, skips, tiling and decoration, floor coverings, supplying bathroom fittings, structural engineers' fees, and planning & building control applications – not forgetting VAT!

To save money you could get specialists to do the groundwork/foundations and structural work, and source builders or individual trades for the rest. But don't just pick any builder from Yellow Pages. Try to source experienced contractors via recommendations, check their previous projects.

Employing non-English-speaking trades can cause communication problems. So for anything other than labouring, it's safer to stick with home-grown trades folk. Apart from a designer, the only professionals you need to employ are a structural engineer at the design stage, and possibly a surveyor for any party wall issues.

* Foundations

It's obviously essential to have proper foundations. Even lightweight, highly glazed extensions need proper foundations. They must not simply be built off a concrete slab, otherwise they'll move with seasonal ground conditions and start to crack.

Building Control will need to approve the design in advance. In most cases standard strip or trenchfill foundations should be acceptable. Typically an excavator will dig a trench about 1.2m deep x 600mm wide, but much will depend on the type of ground you're building on, e.g. clay, chalk, gravel or chalk. In areas with clay subsoils trees up to 20 metres away can affect foundations, so depths may therefore need to be greater – sometimes as much 2.5 metres. In very poor ground you may be asked to use more expensive raft foundations or piles, so on a tight budget this needs to be agreed early on.

* Walls

Conventional cavity masonry walls are normally the simplest and most economical construction method. These might comprise an inner leaf of (thermally efficient) blockwork with an outer leaf of brick or blockwork which could be rendered or perhaps clad with timber weatherboarding or tile hung. Stainless steel (or plastic) wall ties hold the 2 leafs together and the cavities are insulated as the work proceeds. Suitable lintels must be installed above all openings to windows and doors etc, and a damp proof course (DPC) incorporated about 2 brick courses above the finished exterior ground level. Normally it's the inner leaf that supports most the loadings from the roof and floors.

* Roofs

Simple flat roofs are the cheapest type to build, typically comprising '8 x 2' softwood joists topped with a plywood deck onto which a felt covering is applied. Decks need to be built with a slope of about 5-10 degrees so that rainwater doesn't 'pond' but runs down to the gutters. This is achieved by placing thin timber wedges known as 'firrings' on top of the joists. Roofs need to be insulated, and the best way to do this is with 100mm thick polyurethane type insulation boards laid on top of the deck before felting. Alternatively mineral wool insulation can be laid between the joists above the ceiling, leaving a 50mm ventilation path above the quilt (and vents at the fascias).

Junctions with the main house walls are critical and felt should be lapped at 'upstands' and tucked into mortar joints, ideally with an independent lead flashing strip covering.

Pitched roofs are simplest (and cheapest) when constructed as a 'lean to' with a single slope of timber rafter construction finished with concrete tiles or artificial slate. Metal flashings should be applied at the abutment with the main house wall or roof. The size of the rafters and any supporting beams will depend on the loadings and spans involved – span tables can be seen at www.home-extension.co.uk. More complex roofs will require design input from a structural engineer.

* Detailing

Where the extension roof joins the main wall of the house, the joint needs to be carefully sealed, as this is potential weak-point for leaks. The best advice is to use traditional lead lead flashings which although relatively expensive are by far the best material. Joints to walls need to allow for some flexibility between the existing house and the new extension (see 'breaking through' below). Also in older houses with suspended timber floors bear in mind that it's important not to block the airbricks that ventilate under the ground floor (as the flow of air helps prevent damp and rot). One solution is to connect them to new airbricks in the lower walls of the extension with ducting laid within the new floor. Getting detailing right is also important with the new damp proof course (DPC) to the extension lower walls (positioned at least 150mm above the ground level). This should be joined up with the old DPC.

* Floors

Ground floors in smaller extensions are often still built the traditional way, of solid concrete. For larger floor areas modern 'beam & block' suspended concrete can be a better option, utilising ready made reinforced concrete joists designed to accommodate concrete blocks as an infill, with insulation laid on top, usually under a screed finish.

Traditional solid concrete ground floors are generally made by excavating the topsoil and compacting down a thick base layer of crushed stone or rubble hardcore. This is smoothed and levelled on top ('blinded') with sand and a 1200g polythene sheet damp proof membrane placed over the sand and lapped into the DPC (damp proof course) in the wall. Rigid insulation boards are then laid on top and concrete poured over the insulation (at least 100mm thick) to form a slab. This can then be float finished or a screed later applied.

Upper floors are generally made from conventional '8 x 2in' softwood joists, or modern manufactured 'I' beams. Upstairs floors will need to include some sound insulation, such as 100mm of mineral wool quilt (loft insulation) placed between joists. Similarly, new internal walls around bedrooms need to be insulated to reduce sound transmission, usually by filling studwork with mineral wool.

* Ventilation

To provide an adequate amount of air to your new rooms, and to help prevent condensation and mould, windows should have inbuilt 'trickle vents'. These are small slots in the tops of frames that you can leave open to provide controllable background ventilation without the need to open windows. But to provide 'rapid ventilation' windows need to have an openable area equivalent to 1/20th of the floor area of the room. And to disperse moist humid air before it can cause damp and condensation indoors, extractor fans must be fitted to bathrooms, cloakrooms, utilities, and kitchens.

* Light

Adding a large extension can make existing reception rooms very dark. One of the most common mistakes is where a new extension on the back of the house, effectively blots out most of the light to the old rear reception / dining room, which then becomes a sort of no man's land that nobody wants to use. So you end up adding a new room but losing an old room.

Fortunately there are a number of ways you can boost the amount of light getting into a building. The simplest approach with single storey extensions is to incorporate skylight roof windows, available both for pitched and flat roofs. These aren't too expensive and fairly easy to install. Other options include 'light tubes' that channel light down from above. With 2 storey extensions getting light down to the ground floor requires careful design – this is where a good architect can really earn their fee. For example the ground floor can be built a bit larger than the first floor bedroom above, with a small subsidiary roof projecting out that can be used for roof lights. Internally it helps if the light isn't blocked by partition walls, so you could perhaps consider glazed stairs and floors (subject to budget!) or simply adding a few glass blocks in the internal walls.

Bear in mind however that there are limits on the amount of glazing you're allowed to include in a new extension. This is to stop it effectively becoming a conservatory, leaking all the heat out of the house. The basic rule is that the new glazing should not exceed an area equivalent to 25% of extension's floor area, plus a bit more to compensate for the loss of any original windows or doors now blocked up.

And as a safety measure, glazing in and around doors, and all glazing within 800mm of the floor must be made either of toughened or laminated glass.

Element	Part L (2010) U-value
Wall	0.28
Floor	0.22
Flat roof	0.18
Pitched roof (warm)	0.18
Pitched roof (cold)	0.16
Doors	1.8
Windows & rooflights	1.6 or WER Band C

PICKING THE RIGHT STYLE

There's no law that says you have to build your extension in the same materials as your house. But to keep costs down in usually makes sense to stick with conventional cavity masonry walls, with the outer leaf of brick or rendered blockwork, and the inner leaf of blockwork. Modern cavity walls tend to be around 300mm thick, including a 100mm wide cavity, which is insulated as it is built. For improved thermal performance (i.e. minimal heat loss) the inner face is usually dry-lined with plasterboard, and you could even opt to clad the outer leaf with rigid insulation boards (at additional cost). A traditional external treatment of tile hanging or weatherboarding is another option.

The second most popular method of construction is modern timber frame, where the inner leaf is manufactured from softwood studwork clad with a sheet material such as plywood or OSB and pre-insulated. The outer leaf is normally of brick or block.

Where money is no object there are 2 appealing alternative options – one from the past and one from future. Respectively these are traditional oak framing and pure glass extensions. In fact it's possible to combine these with high-performance glazing used as infill panels between oak posts and beams.

As we saw earlier, there are limits to the area of glazing you're allowed to include in your new extension (up to 25% of extension's floor area + a bit for any old windows or doors now blocked up).This is obviously a concern if you want to use a lot of glass in your new design. Fortunately there are 2 ways you can get around this restriction and justify higher levels of glazing :-

a. Trade off
By super-insulating the other thermal elements of your new extension you should then be able to demonstrate that the average ('area weighted') Energy Performance for the whole extension is no worse than if the design complied with the 25% rule (subject to meeting minimum threshold U-values).

b. Upgrade the whole house

Here you need to prove that the combined energy performance of the extension PLUS that of the main house – *once upgraded* – will be no worse in total than if you built a standard extension on the house as it stands.

PROBLEM SOLVING

There are a number of tricky issues that you may come up against when building an extension. Thinking about these in advance can save a lot of hassle and expense later. Fortunately, there are a number of possible solutions:-

What if there's an obstruction in the way?

To avoid the nightmare scenario of smashing into underground drain runs it's obviously a good idea to locate them before you start building. But old plans and records held by water companies can be surprisingly inaccurate. Even for recently constructed buildings where the developers or the local authority have retained copies of the original drawings, the actual layout sometimes bears little relation to that shown on the plans.

Where there are no records, a simple drain survey can be carried out to help trace the route of underground pipework. Starting in the main bathroom, locate the main soil & vent pipe (SVPs are the large vertical waste pipes run externally on most pre 1960s houses or boxed-in internally in more modern properties). From the base of the SVP draw a line to the nearest inspection chamber (manhole).

Do the same from the base of any hoppers and downpipes channelling waste water from upstairs bathrooms. Lift the cover and work outwards from the house to other chambers, measuring their position and noting any branch pipes and gulleys serving kitchens, cloakrooms and utilities. In cases where there's little or no surface evidence, the age of the property can sometimes provide clues to the whereabouts of hidden drain runs and experimental trial holes carefully excavated by hand. Victorian terraces often have a shared sewer running across the back gardens connected to a branch pipe from each property. In 1930s semis the drains usually run parallel to the side wall leading out to the sewer in the street. Later properties were often designed with the kitchens and bathrooms to the front so the drains could run straight out to the main system in the road.

You also need to consider how surface water is discharged noting the position of downpipes. But diverting surface water is usually more straightforward. For example it may be possible to channel existing pipes via the roof of the new extension into a new downpipe, gulley and soakaway.

Who's responsibility is it?
Homeowners are only responsible for foul waste pipes located within the boundaries serving just their own home ('private drains'). Where your pipework runs under next door's garden (a 'lateral drain') it becomes the responsibility of the water company. Public ownership commences at the point where a drain becomes shared, serving more than one property (ie becomes a sewer) or where it passes across the boundary and under the public highway. For properties with private systems such as septic tanks, responsibility for the whole system lies with the homeowners.

Building over a public sewer or lateral drain can be a major undertaking (both are the responsibility of the water authority). Even building within 3 metres of a sewer normally requires official consent. So when designing your extension there are 3 options:-

a. Avoid the sewer: normally the easiest and cheapest solution is to modify your plans so the extension will be at least 3 metres away from the sewer.

b. Divert the sewer: where practical you could divert the sewer away from where you want to build. Small drains connecting one or two households to a sewer are usually fairly easy to divert (subject to agreement), but larger sewers cannot readily be moved.

c. Build over it (or within 3 metres). Water companies have a right of access to sewers located on private property so their consent will be required to build an extension over the top. This normally requires entering into a 'building-over agreement' with the water company who will then carry out a preliminary CCTV survey to check its condition prior to building work. Once the extension is completed, a follow-up CCTV scan will check whether any damage has been caused by the works - with any repairs charged to you. Pipes passing through walls can be protected by installing a lintel above the opening, leaving a gap of at least 50mm around the pipe to allow for any settlement.

Re-siting drains & inspection chambers

As a rule, underground drainage systems should be accessible without the need to enter buildings. However where a chamber only serves a single dwelling, internal access may be permitted subject to it being fitted with a special airtight cover. Otherwise Building Control are likely to require that your extension is redesigned or the drains diverted.

The bulk of the cost of diverting drain runs is in the excavation, so combining this with digging the foundations can reap significant economies. Modern ready-made plastic inspection units are inexpensive (from around £50) and can be used as a substitute for older full-sized brickwork inspection chambers. Where space is very limited Building Control may instead accept compact rodding eyes.

Trees

Where there are trees nearby, cutting through roots during excavating work could destabilise them with potentially serious consequences. To avoid severing the main roots (normally those greater than 50mm diameter) trenches can be hand-excavated rather than using a mini digger. Where encroachment of roots is severe removal of the tree may be the only option. But this can have implications for ground conditions (and hence foundation design) due to the reduction in moisture extraction. Any tree removal should be disclosed as part of the planning application.
To protect underground drainage pipes from future growth a 'root barrier' can be constructed between the pipe run and the offending trees. This is a physical 'shield' in the ground in the form of a deep, narrow trench filled with concrete or special rigid plastic sheeting.

Extending above a garage or an existing single storey extension

Building new accommodation on top of an existing single storey extension or an attached garage can make a lot of sense from a design point of view. But the extra loadings imposed can be as much as 3 tonnes per metre of foundation, so how can you ensure that the old structure you're building onto is capable of supporting the additional load?

The good news is, most extensions built in the last 25 years or so should have sufficiently deep foundations to accommodate the addition of an extra storey at a later date – assuming they complied with Building Regulations. If there are no records to confirm this, trial holes will need to be dug to assess the quality, depth and thickness of the existing foundations in relation to the type of subsoil. Adding new loadings will also amplify any hidden weaknesses in the existing structure, so lintels and beams subject to increased loads should also be checked.

Building over garages is rarely a practical proposition without substantial additional support because of their very limited load-bearing capacity. Even relatively modern garages usually have thin 115mm walls interspersed with the occasional brick pier, and many others are little more than tumble-down shacks. In marginal cases, Building Control might accept a new lightweight first floor structure, perhaps of timber frame and cladding, subject to engineer's calculations.

Where an old structure isn't up to the job there are a number of options. Underpinning existing shallow foundations is rarely feasible because of the cost – typically around £ 1000 per metre run. Alternatively it may be possible to strengthen the old structure, or bypass it entirely by erecting a new framework with steel posts bedded in new concrete pad footings.

Where the existing ground floor building is very basic, the best option is normally to demolish it and start from scratch (you may be able to re-use some materials or retaining the floor slab). This way you'll benefit from ground floor accommodation that is properly built and fully insulated, rather than having to refurbish the old sub-standard structure.

Breaking through and joining up

The traditional method for tying-in a new extension to the existing house is by 'toothing in' each course of brickwork. This involves hacking away every other brick at the interface with the main building and slotting in matching new ones to make a seamless connection – assuming that your new bricks were a perfect match in size with each course neatly aligned. But there's a major risk with this method - 'differential settlement' can occur where a new extension with deep, super-strong foundations is joined to an older property on shallower footings, with resulting cracking between the two structures.

To overcome such problems, flexible 'wall starter systems' (known as 'crocodiles') can accommodate around 10mm of vertical movement. These comprise vertical strips of stainless steel fixed to the existing wall with expansion bolts, one abutting each leaf of the new cavity wall. Projecting anchor ties are bedded every 2 or 3 courses into the mortar joints of the new brickwork. Variations in courses can be accommodated because the ties are adjustable. The resulting vertical joint to the outer brickwork should be filled with a compressible seal (or flexible mastic or polymer based pointing). Joints can be camouflaged with strategically placed downpipes, cladding, or door openings.

The potential for movement and cracking also needs to be considered where extensions are constructed from different materials to those of the property they're being built onto, because of the variance in performance characteristics. However extensions built using modern construction methods such as SIPS and ICFs are generally clad externally with a brick or blockwork outer leaf, similarly to conventional timber frame construction, which means standard wall connector systems can normally be used.

A similar dilemma can arise where you're joining a new masonry extension to a house of non-standard construction. In most cases this will involve homes of post war Council origin (such as PRC, steel frame or concrete panels). Because properties of this type are not generally accepted by mortgage lenders unless suitably upgraded, most will by now have been re-clad with a masonry outer leaf, again making it feasible for extensions to be connected conventionally. Differential movement between old and new structures is a particularly factor with extensions built from of traditional green oak framing, as the design needs to accommodate substantial initial movement at the interface as the oak dries out and hardens. But probably the most challenging combination is where rigid, pure glass wall panels need to be tied-in to an older building prone to seasonal movement on shallow foundations, requiring the use of specialist flexible jointing systems.

When it comes to 'breaking through' to provide access to the new extension, in houses on non-standard construction, it's best to make use of existing door openings (or windows cut away below sill level) to avoid disrupting supporting structures such as steel posts.

As noted earlier, at roof level it's especially important to achieve an effective seal at the interface with the new extension. A traditional lead flashing is normally sufficient to accommodate movement at the joint between the two structures, but should have a generous upstand (minimum 150mm) and wedged into a raked out 10mm slot in the wall above and pointed up.

Extending the electrics
The first question to ask when extending an electrical circuit is whether your existing system is able to cope with the additional load. Properties dating from the 1970s or earlier with their original wiring will by now be overdue for complete renewal. And if your consumer unit (distribution board) is an older type with rewireable fuses it will need to be replaced. Modern 'split load' consumer units have MCB' s (miniature circuit breakers) for each individual circuit and additional RCD (residual current device) protection, massively reducing the risk of electric shocks and fire.

The power circuits supplying the socket outlets in the walls and are arranged in a loop or 'ring main'. One circuit can normally serve a floor area up to 100m2 (an average 3 bed semi having 50 to 60m2 floor area for each storey) but any number of power points can be provided within this. So it's normally possible to extend the existing ring circuit unless the wiring is very dated or the new accommodation is unusually vast. For larger extensions a new independent circuit can be run from the consumer unit (most modern units should have sufficient spare capacity).

Kitchens are high demand areas and need their own dedicated circuit. So if your extension is for a new kitchen, this could be served by a new supply run direct from the consumer unit. Alternatively you could extend the cable supplying the (soon to be redundant) existing kitchen. Electric cookers and immersion heaters also require separate fused circuits; and cables run to outdoors should have their own mini consumer unit.
Lighting systems are also typically arranged with one circuit supplying each floor, although new lighting circuits may also need to incorporate smoke alarms and shaver points.

All new electrical work must comply with Part P of the Building Regulations which severely restricts DIY electrical work. Electricians can normally self-certify their installations if they're registered with a body that gives them the necessary 'registered installer' status. Upon completion of the job, it is a legal requirement for the electrician to test the new system and hand over a signed BS 7671 electrical safety certificate.

Extending the heating system
When you're adding extra living space it's important to know whether the current heating system will be able to cope with the additional load. The first thing to check is the age of your boiler – older ones may be due for replacement fairly soon (modern boilers typically last no more than 15 to 20 years). Check also whether you've got a combination boiler that provides both heating and instant hot water, because 'combis' will generally struggle to supply an additional bathroom.

Assuming your boiler has passed these first two tests, the next step is to assess whether it's up to the job of supplying your newly extended home. Calculating the optimum boiler size for the enlarged property is done by totalling the output of all the radiators and adding a bit for hot water requirements (typically about 2 kW) to give a figure for the total heat required. The industry standard is to design heating systems capable of heating the whole house around 21 degrees C warmer than the temperature outside. The optimum size for each radiator to provide sufficient heat for the room will depend on factors such as room size and the thermal efficiency of the house. A template for calculating this can be found at www.sedbuk.com where you can also check the efficiency of your existing boiler.

Boilers are rated by the power they produce in either 'BTUs' (British Thermal Units) or kilowatts (1kW = 3,410 BTU). As a rough guide, a 50,000 BTU boiler should be capable of heating a typical 3 bedroom house with 10 radiators plus a hot water cylinder. But a large poorly insulated Victorian house might require something like 100,000 BTUs (30 kW).

Another factor to consider is whether the location of the boiler flue clashes with the new extension; if it does, the boiler will need to be moved or the flue diverted. However with modern condensing boilers the flues can sometimes be extended upwards or sideways, so there may be a simpler solution. By law, alterations to heating systems and fitting appliances must be carried out by suitably qualified heating engineers registered with Gas Safe for gas fired boilers or OFTEC for oil fired boilers, although there's nothing to stop you doing the hot and cold water pipework on a DIY basis.

Replacing your boiler can make a big difference to reducing the amount of energy consumed in the home. But what are the alternatives if your existing model is working at full capacity but is nowhere near its sell-by date? One option would be to fit a small additional combi boiler just to supply the extension, but this would be relatively expensive with significant longer term overheads running and maintaining two boilers.

Fitting modern programmable controls and TRVs to your existing system makes sense as it can slash the cost of running the central heating by up to 30%. Combined with upgraded insulation to improve the thermal efficiency of your property, this could free up sufficient spare capacity to provide the necessary additional space heating. The demand placed on the boiler could be further reduced by replacing an old hot water cylinder with an efficient mains-fed pressurised system; ideally this could be combined with a new solar thermal hot water installation on the extension roof, typically costing around £4800 (*source:* Energy Saving Trust).

A well insulated new extension might only require 10 to 15 watts per cubic metre of living space, so the extra demand may not be particularly high. This could make fixed electric storage heaters a realistic option. But although cheap to install, these offer relatively little control and are one of the more expensive systems to run. In a well insulated extension, a better option might be underfloor heating (UFH). 'Dry systems' take the form of ultra-thin flexible mats containing electric heating elements that can be laid directly under floor coverings such as ceramic tiles and are ideal for background heating. But again they are relatively expensive to run and best suited to smaller areas such as cloakrooms and en-suites. More popular for new extensions are 'wet' UFH systems where warm water is pumped at low pressure through concealed pipework buried in the floor screed. Although dearer to install than standard radiator systems, UFH is more energy efficient since it works at relatively low temperatures (10 to 15 degrees).

Access issues

Extending a mid terraced house with restricted access to the garden can have major practical implications when carrying out building work. Builders' quotes will normally factor-in the extra hassle where access and parking are awkward, potentially adding as much as 5% to the overall cost. However a 'work around' solution can sometimes be devised to keep costs down. Many older terraces have a shared right of way running across all the back gardens from a side road or alleyway. Others have an unmade service road or pathway to the rear (minimum 3m width is normally required for vehicular access). Otherwise if you're on good terms with neighbours in an end terrace property it may be possible to agree temporary access via their garden.

If all else fails materials and equipment will need to be laboriously carted through the house, having first taken the necessary measures to protect floors, fittings and wall finishes.

Careful planning is required to ensure the ready-mixed concrete wagon has a sufficiently extendable pumping hose (some are as short as 17 metres). Also the dimensions of large plant such as cement mixers will need to be checked in advance. On the plus side, site security shouldn't be much of a problem!

The design will need to take account of restricted access, ruling out large prefabricated components like roof trusses. However where the cost is justified large items such as large glass wall panels can be physically craned in over the top of the house.

Probably the biggest challenge isn't so much getting stuff in, but getting excavated waste out, barrowing it through the hall on scaffold planks. The smaller the site, the more critical it is to get rid of excavated earth and waste at regular intervals, otherwise work can soon grind to a halt. Some waste such as excavated topsoil and broken bricks can be re-used, saving the cost and hassle of disposing of it.Staggering delivery times can help avoid overcrowding the site with mountains of materials all arriving at once. But if deliveries have to be delayed because of a lack of space you could end up paying trades to sit around doing nothing.

Structural issues with party walls
Structural issues can potentially arise where you need to excavate trenches for foundations or drains in close proximity to next door's property. Alarm bells should ring if, for example, the neighbours have got a cheap DIY conservatory or a decrepit outbuilding nearby that will be super-sensitive to the slightest ground movement. Where you need to carry out excavations in such high risk areas, to avoid subsequent disputes a structural engineer should first be consulted to assess the ground conditions and decide whether special precautions are needed such as temporary shoring up.

To accommodate these sorts of risks from a legal perspective the Party Wall Act applies when excavating within 3 metres of an adjacent property where your new foundations are deeper than those next door. It can also potentially apply within 6 metres of another building – but only if your new foundations are deeper than a theoretical line drawn at 45 degrees from the bottom of next door's foundations, for example where you're building a new basement or using deep pile foundations. In such cases you normally need to appoint a Party Wall surveyor to manage the process.

Where the neighbour has already built an extension along your garden boundary, you may need to build up to it, so their side wall becomes the new party wall separating the two extensions. Any fixing into next door's existing wall will obviously need to be done with great care, and in compliance with the Party Wall Act. You will also need to ensure that the wall has adequate sound resistance and meets the necessary one hour fire resistance standard (a conventional masonry wall should exceed this).

3.
Adding a Conservatory

Conservatories are a relatively inexpensive way of adding extra space, as budget-priced home extensions. But it's a false economy to cut corners so you end up with a leaky greenhouse stuck on the back of your house. So in this chapter we look at where you can genuinely save money and when it's worth going the extra mile to achieve an attractive and useful space.

At their simplest, conservatories comprise some form of a glazed framework built upon a simple concrete slab (over a base of compacted crushed hardcore). If money is really tight, kits are available that can be bolted together in a day. On the plus side you get extra space at minimal cost, perhaps coming in useful as somewhere to stashing kids' toys etc. But the basic quality will make it unusable for much of the year – freezing in winter and unbearably hot in summer. It will also be prone to condensation, movement and staggering amounts of heat loss. Which makes it very expensive storage space.

In contrast, at the upper end of the market, bespoke 'orangeries' employ super-thermally efficient 'low-E' double or triple glazing set within high performance insulated frames, built upon substantial masonry base walls. Which is all very nice, but the cost will then be on a par with building a 'proper' extension, which would provide more useful space (such as a kitchen/diner) as well as being better insulated with smaller expanses of glazing.

QUESTIONS TO ASK UP FRONT

* Can you extend without planning permission? In most cases the answer is 'yes' – see Permitted Development Rights below. However you may still need to make a Building Regulations application.

* Is my house suitable? Some houses are easier to adapt than others - it helps if you don't have obstacles that need diverting, like boilers and drainage pipes.

* What will it cost? You won't know for sure without getting quotes but there are lots of ways to keep the price down – see 'doing it on a budget' below.

Minimising disturbance
You don't want your home to be overwhelmed by the building works. So it's important to arrange things so that life can carry on as normal.

* Access for labour and materials can cause enormous disruption. This can be tricky in terraced houses where there's no side gate to the garden, but there are ways this can be resolved – see 'Access Issues' in the previous chapter under 'Problem Solving'.

* Deliveries: So that building materials can be delivered and safely stored it's a good idea to allocate space in advance – or they'll just get dumped somewhere incredibly inconvenient.

* To minimise dust and noise it's best to leave cutting any new openings from the house as long as possible. You might also want to agree some things in advance with the builders such as the time work starts on site each day.

* Services: The existing electrical systems will normally need to be extended for lighting and for the ring main plug circuit. It's best to schedule a day for this work when the main supply can be temporarily cut off without causing too much disruption.

* Loo breaks: you might want to protect your carpet with sheets so builders can utilise the facilities – or hire a handy port-a-loo.

You can buy reasonable quality DIY conservatory kits for around £4,000. This would typically be sized about 10 sq metres (about 3.5 x 3 metres) with a pitched roof. However you will need to add the cost of foundations, building a 600mm dwarf wall, and the floor structure & finish, plus lead flashings. So you'd probably be looking at spending nearer £7,000 in total.

A typical basic kit would comprise a 70mm PVCu frame with 24mm Low 'E' double safety glass panels, 2 opening windows (with lockable handles), French doors, and a pitched roof frame with 25mm polycarbonate sheet roofing.

PLANNING & BUILDING REGS

Planning rules are basically the same as for extensions. But when it comes to the Building Regulations there are some very specific rules that need to be complied with. At face value these can seem unnecessarily fussy (things like not extending the heating system to add an extra radiator in the conservatory) until you consider the enormous potential for heat loss in cold weather.

Planning applications

Conservatories can very often be built without the need for a planning application. This is thanks to the Permitted Development Rules (PDRs) that are discussed in some detail in the previous chapter. Of course this 'free allowance' is subject to meeting a number of conditions, and may not apply to some properties, in which case a planning application will be required - so always check with your local Council at the design stage.

In terms of floor area most conservatories are no larger then about 12 sq metres - typically about 3 metres deep and about 4 metres wide. This might have something to do with the fact that PDR rules (until recently when they were temporarily doubled – see previous chapter) allowed a maximum depth to the rear of the house of 3 metres (or 4 metres for detached houses). Either way, there is a height limit of 4 metres and the width should be no wider than the existing rear elevation of the house. Which, when you think about it, is extraordinarily generous.

Building Regulations

Where a conservatory doesn't meet the necessary Building Regulations criteria, it will be classed as a 'highly glazed extension' or a 'garden room' and will need to fully comply as a home extension. This is a real game changer because, as we saw in the previous chapter, there are strict limits on how much glazing you can include in extensions, and even stricter rules on efficiency standards requiring super-high levels of insulation.

However conservatories are **exempt** from the Building Regulations provided they meet certain criteria:-

* The internal floor area has a maximum size limit of 30 m2.

* Not less than 75% of the roof and 50% of the walls should comprise a transparent or translucent material - either glass or polycarbonate sheeting.

* All critical and low-level glazing should comprise safety glass – i.e. glazing below 1500mm in height in doors (or within 300mm of a door) must be toughened or laminated, as must all glazing below 800mm in height, e.g. to doors. Window sill heights should be a minimum 800mm above floor level.

* Conservatories must be thermally separated from the main house with exterior quality doors (including patio or French doors).

* Any new heater or radiator must not be linked to your existing central heating system in the house. Portable heaters are acceptable. Or if you want to install a fixed heating system such as new underfloor heating or radiators they must be independent from the rest of the house and capable of being controlled separately, so they can be set to a lower temperature or turned completely off.

* Where the conservatory blocks the windows/doors to a habitable room, it should be able to provide sufficient ventilation for both rooms. So conservatory doors and opening windows should in total be no smaller than 1/20th of the combined floor area of both rooms. Plus you need background ventilation of at least 8000mm2. The closable openings separating the conservatory from the house need to meet similar size and ventilation requirements.

* Conservatories must be located at ground level – i.e, not built on a balcony or on top of an extension!

Even with all the above boxes ticked, there are some other areas where the Building Regulations could potentially still apply:-

* Where the structure is built over a shared drain run (something that must be checked before excavating!). N.B. you are not allowed to build over a Public Sewer – to find out if there are any Public Sewers on your property check with your local Water Authority.

* Any new electrical circuits (lighting or power) must comply with Part P of the Building Regulations, so the work should normally be carried out by a 'Competent Person'.

* Any structural alterations, such as a new opening from the house to the conservatory will require Building Regulations approval, even if the conservatory itself is an exempt building.

Danger! Heat loss
Adding a conservatory to create a large open plan kitchen/diner can be create a pleasant, bright feel. But without any dividing doors to separate it from the main house, much of your room heat will be sucked straight out of the house via the conservatory, sending energy bills rocketing. In fact heating a conservatory to the same level as a normal room can double a household energy bill! (source: Ovo Energy). Hence the requirement for having 'exterior quality' doors to the house.

Simple polycarbonate roofs can allow more than 15 times the amount of heat to escape than conventional tiled roofs. In summer the opposite problem can occur, as the sun heats the enclosed space to unbearable temperatures. So where there is no thermal separation from the house, garden rooms must be designed so they don't leak heat. Which, as noted above, means the Building Regs treat them as extensions and the design will need to meet very demanding thermal efficiency requirements (Part L).

When it comes to designing your conservatory, there are some general points to bear in mind.

* Better quality designs have low level base walls of cavity masonry construction laid to normal foundation depths, upon which the superstructure is fixed – as opposed to simply being erected upon a thin concrete slab (which can lead to problems with structural movement and damp).

* Flues serving wall-mounted boilers are often located so they clash with the proposed conservatory. This normally means having to relocate the boiler so the flue is well clear of the building. But with modern condensing boilers the flues can sometimes be extended upwards or sideways, so there may be a simpler solution – check with a heating engineer.

* Ventilated roof ridges should be incorporated to relieve air pressure and prevent 'wind uplift' that can push out lightweight roof panels.

* Try to avoid building the conservatory where it could hamper rescue by ladder in the event of fire to windows serving loft rooms.

* Getting the detailing right particularly at junction with the house is important to prevent leaks etc – the same advice applies as described earlier for building extensions - see 'Problem Solving' below.

* Floor levels in conservatory are often built lower than those of the house. This isn't a good idea because low level floors are an invitation for surface water from the garden to enter, making the new accommodation potentially vulnerable to flooding (although raised door thresholds can help). Note that new floor should not block air bricks to the lower walls of houses with timber floors; these will need to be channelled with ducting through the new floor (as described for extensions).

PROBLEM SOLVING

Many of the challenges you face when adding new conservatories are essentially the same as for building extensions. The following issues are covered in more detail the previous chapter:-

What if there's an obstruction in the way?

It's not unusual to find there's a rainwater downpipe just where you want to park your gleaming new addition. However this needn't be a problem because it's usually a simple matter to divert downpipes into the new guttering on the conservatory. Of course the diverted rainwater will then need to disperse via a new downpipe from the conservatory. This will probably mean having to excavate a trench for a new underground pipe leading safely away (at least 5 metres) so water can be channelled out to a soakaway in the garden or handy ditch etc. Excavation can be done at the same time as the foundations using a mini digger.

In older houses there's often a soil & vent pipe (SVP) on the back or side wall taking foul waste from the bathroom. These can often be incorporated within the conservatory and boxed in. Where you need to build over underground drainage pipes, they can be bridged over with a simple concrete lintel. But in some cases a 'building over agreement' may be needed, and the need for any re-siting of inspection chambers and drain runs is best avoided – see previous chapter.

Breaking through and joining up

Tying-in a new conservatory to the existing house requires a flexible watertight joint to accommodate any future movement between the 2 structures. It's particularly important to fit a generous lead flashing at roof abutments to adjoining walls. Any openings for pipes etc projecting through roofs will also need to be carefully sealed with flashings. When it comes to providing access from the house into the new conservatory, in most cases an existing door opening (patio or French doors) can be utilised or an existing window opening deepened to form a new doorway. This rules out the need for structural work making openings wider or cutting new ones. Keeping the existing lintel in place saves a lot of dust and mess, as well the need for Building Regs approval for new structural work.

Extending the electrics

The existing electrical system will need to be extended to provide new lighting and possibly a few power sockets, but the additional demand shouldn't impose much in the way of loadings. However, if you plan to run some form of electric heater (e.g. storage heater) a new heavy duty independent supply cable will be required.

Although most DIY electrical work is restricted under Part P of the Building Regulations, running a single spur socket extension or a single new light may in some cases be acceptable – check with Building Control.

Electricians can normally self-certify their installations if they're registered with a body that gives them the necessary 'registered installer' status. Upon completion of the job, it is a legal requirement for the electrician to test the new system and hand over a signed BS 7671 electrical safety certificate.

Structural issues with party walls

Structural issues can potentially arise where you need to excavate trenches for foundations or drains in close proximity to next door's property. To accommodate these sorts of risks from a legal perspective the Party Wall Act applies when excavating within 3 metres of an adjacent property where your new foundations are deeper than those next door.

4.
Garage Conversions
'an extra room in 10 days'

For most homeowners, garages are a waste of space. Whilst cars have grown ever larger, housebuilders continue to erect slender 'size zero' garages typically measuring a miniscule 2.7 m x 5.8 metres – including the walls. Which is fine if you drive a Reliant Robin. So with our homes bursting at the seams it's no wonder that thousands of garages are now finding a new incarnation as extra rooms.

Single garages typically provide about 12 sq metres of useable floor area, and because the shell is already there, they can be relatively cheap to convert to living space – typically less than a quarter of the price of building the equivalent extension or loft room. Garage conversions are also a lot quicker to build - typically taking about 10 to 14 days for a single, compared to as long as 3 to 6 months an extension - and with far less mess and hassle.

So the only real obstacle between you and a spacious new lifestyle is likely to be the periodic occupant - traditionally the male of the species - who may require some gentle persuasion to vacate the premises. Fortunately, most of the old paint pots, bits of broken furniture and ancient gearboxes should fit handsomely into a new garden shed. Or even better, you could flog them to help finance the project.

QUESTIONS TO ASK UP FRONT

* Is my garage suitable?   Regrettably, not all garages are ripe for conversion. The easiest type to transform are integral garages or those attached to the house. Plus, the older they are, the less chance of them having proper (or any) foundations. If you're the proud owner of an old curiosity lurking somewhere down the garden, its potential may be fairly limited. Many old garages are often little more than tumble-down shacks with walls of paper-thin brick, block or crumbing prefabricated panels sheltering under leaky felt roofs or dodgy asbestos sheeting. In such cases the simplest option is often to demolish and rebuild. So let's assume you're starting with a structurally sound, reasonably modern garage. Nonetheless, the first job is always to check the condition of the structure, keeping an eye open for cracks, damp patches and roof leaks etc.

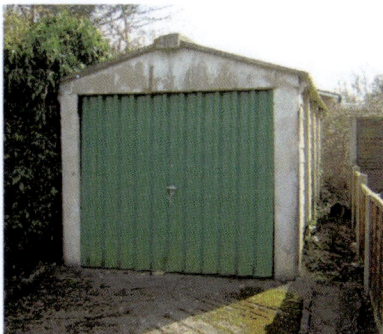

* Access: How will you get into the new room? Is there an internal doorway from the house, or could one potentially be provided?

* Do I need planning permission? In most cases the answer is 'no' – see Permitted Development Rights below. However you will still need to make a Building Regulations application (also discussed below).

* Parking: Conversion only really makes sense where you have alternative space for parking, such as to the front garden. Or if you live in a quiet backwater, parking in the street may suffice. But gaining a new room at the expense of endless parking tickets means you could actually be detracting from the marketability of your property. Parking is at a premium in many cities where local councils may refuse planning for otherwise acceptable conversions.

What is considered an acceptable level of parking provision will depend on the type of property. For flats and smaller houses a couple of car spaces is usually considered sufficient. For larger family homes, either integral or attached garages are the norm. At the upper end of the market cavernous detached doubles and even triples are desirable.

Will it add value?
The amount of value added by an improvement depends on the extent to which it overcomes a major negative, such as a tiny kitchen. But if it's gained at the expense of losing something else, in this case the garage, whether it adds value or not can be a bit of a grey area - with half the market liking the extra space, but the other half regretting not having a garage.

One option is to hedge your bets by converting just the back part, thereby retaining some storage space. Double garages are often divided in half with the side nearest the house upgraded for accommodation and one bay kept for parking.

What will it cost?
Unlike loft conversions and extensions this can be a realistic project for competent DIY enthusiasts, with major savings thanks to cutting out the labour costs and the contractor's profit margin. By doing some of the work yourself it should be possible to carry out a conversion for less than about £ 6000. But if you don't have the time or inclination for DIY, employing a specialist garage conversion company to do the whole thing as a package deal may be a better, if more expensive option.

Specialist conversion firms offer a 'one stop shop' service with everything included. The quoted price should include all the necessary drawings and fees for local authority consents, and a Building Control completion certificate must be provided at the end of the job. Typical prices vary from about £10,000 to £15,000 for a single garage (about £700 - £800 per m2 for a single, or £1100 per m2 for a double). But before proceeding, think carefully about exactly what you want, including the position of all the sockets and radiators, as changing your mind later can be expensive.

Alternatively, if you want to manage the job yourself but don't feel confident about some of the technical stuff, a local architect can be employed to produce drawings and a specification for the Building Control application.

Minimising disturbance

Because most of the building work will be carried out away from the habitable parts of the house, this is one improvement that shouldn't intrude too much on your home life. The main flashpoints are likely to come when a new internal door needs to be knocked through to the main house, and the electrics or heating systems are extended. Here are a few points worth pondering before work starts:-

* Access: Unless there's a separate side or rear external door to the garage, to minimise disturbance it's a good idea to leave the installation of the new front window to the main garage door/front wall until as late as possible to provide access for building work from the front.

* Deliveries: So that building materials can be delivered and safely stored it's a good idea to allocate space in advance.

* Services: The existing electrical and heating systems will normally need to be extended. It's best to schedule a day for this work when the main supplies can be temporarily cut off without causing too much disruption.

* Party walls: If any of your garage walls are attached to a neighbouring property, you will need to get a Party Wall agreement drawn up, usually requiring the services of a chartered surveyor.

PLANNING & BUILDING REGS

Planning

You do not normally need planning permission to convert an integral or attached garage into living accommodation. This is because in most cases garage rooms come under the 'Permitted Development Rules', provided the work is internal and you're not making the existing building physically larger, or where it might cause parking problems (only around 20% of conversions require planning consent). But there are exceptions to the rule. It is not unusual for recently built houses to be subject to planning conditions (or restrictive covenants) applied when the property was built, specifically restricting any change of use of the garage. So it's normally advisable to contact the planners at the outset, as local interpretations of the rules vary and in some cases they may be classed as a 'change of use'.

For Listed buildings, the listing also covers garages and outbuildings, so any alterations (including those internally) need consent. For properties in Conservation Areas external visual changes to the front ('principal elevation') will need permission. If you do find yourself hitting planning turbulence, one option is to 'keep it secret' by retaining the existing front elevation with the new living space tucked behind a stud wall and a 'dummy' garage door. This way, no one walking past will ever know! It also makes it easier to reinstate the garage should you find yourself selling the property one day to a dedicated petrol-head.

Building Regulations

There are a number of areas in which garage conversions need to comply with the Building Regs, so Building Control must be notified in advance of the work. This includes upgrading thermal insulation to walls, roofs, floors and windows so that the room is snug and doesn't leak energy, plus the provision of ventilation to prevent condensation. Then in some cases old walls or roofs may need to be upgraded externally to ensure they are fully weather resistant. Other areas where the Building Regulations could potentially apply include:-

* New windows

* Any new drainage connections

* Any necessary foundations to the new front wall

* New electrical circuits (lighting or power)

DESIGN MATTERS

There's a lot more to designing a successful garage conversion than you might imagine. Cheap jobs sometimes fail to conceal the room's utilitarian origins, exuding a stark, narrow feel.

Detached garages that are located fairly close to to the main house can often be linked up with it via a small extension - perhaps a stylish highly glazed job. Or it may be possible to build on top, retaining the existing garage space. Here we look at the main design challenges:-

* Partial conversions

Where you want a new room, but you also need to retain some storage space, it can be a good compromise to do a partial conversion. By converting just the back part of the garage you can leave the front portion and the main door intact. The main challenge is how to get daylight into the new room, for example via a new window to the side.

A partial conversion can also help overcome the inherent problem with single garages that the internal dimensions can appear relatively long and narrow. Retaining part in its original state will curtail the length – problem solved. Or to achieve a more natural 'room shape' you could equally convert it into 2 rooms, perhaps using the smaller space as a cloakroom or shower. Or the space beyond a new partition wall could perhaps be used to enlarge an adjoining utility room or kitchen.

Double garages are particularly well suited to subdivision, and can be divided in half – perhaps helping to preserve marital harmony with the best of both worlds, gaining new living space whilst retaining a place to mess about with engines! However this means that the new internal dividing wall between the living space and the remaining garage will need to comply with fire safety standards, and can either be of conventional blockwork or of timber studwork clad with 2 layers of 12.5mm plasterboard (preferably fireboard) with a skim plaster finish.
Any dividing door must also be fire-rated (min FD30) with intumescent seals and a self-closer. The new floor in the living space should be raised, with a step down into the remaining garage area of at least 100mm.

* Walls

The most straightforward type of garage to convert are those built integrally as part of the house, because the walls should already be of a decent thickness – usually cavity walls. Some modern detached garages also have pukka cavity walls. Where these aren't already insulated, they can be injected with cavity wall insulation.
Attached or 'stand alone' types can be more of a challenge, but much will depend on the age. Most garages that were built by the original developers along with the house should be feasible, particularly those dating from the 1980s or later.
The first task is to check the walls for stability and defects. In most cases the walls will only be of relatively thin 105mm thick single brickwork, supported every 2 metres or so with brick piers (columns). Because rain can potentially penetrate single thickness brickwork, they may need to be treated to resist moisture, e.g. with external wall cladding or a waterproofing compound applied to their inner face. Even if the walls are made from thicker 225mm solid brick, they will still need lining with insulation. Although usually applied internally, it's more effective to clad walls on the outside with thick insulation boards – but this tends to involve a lot of awkward detailing work at windows, doors and downpipes etc, as well as having to extend the roof overhang.

Thermal insulation

From an insulation point of view, these thin walls will need major upgrading to meet the thermal performance target U-value of 0.31 W/m2K.

The general approach to single thickness brickwork is to construct a new treated timber studwork inner leaf, built off 2 courses of engineering bricks (with a new DPC) leaving a 50mm wide cavity. This framework is then packed with 70mm insulation boards and clad with 12.5mm thick plasterboard, having first applied a vapour barrier sheet over the insulation on its 'warm' inner face. Note that the usable width of the room will shrink by about 100mm.

Another way to achieve the recommended thermal performance is by attaching 25mm treated timber battens to the wall (assuming it is free from damp) and lining them with min 60mm thick rigid phenolic foam insulation, before lining with a plastic sheet vapour barrier and plasterboarding (12.5mm thick) - or you could use ready made combined 'insulated plasterboard' totalling 72.5mm thickness).

Alternatively, given that the roof loadings are taken by the existing wall, it should be possible to build a new inner skin of lightweight *thermalite* blocks (concrete floor slabs should normally be able to support the extra load) again leaving a 50mm cavity. Either the cavity can be insulated as the wall is built (where the existing outer face is not prone to damp), or an additional layer of insulation board applied to the new inner face to achieve the required U-value.

The front wall
When it comes to replacing the main garage door with a new infill wall and window (see 'garage doors' below) Building Control may either accept a concrete lintel spanning the opening, or could judge it necessary to excavate new foundations.
To keep damp at bay, if there isn't a damp proof course (DPC) already, the walls must have a new one installed about 150mm above external ground levels, and any earth or paving banked up against the walls removed.

Sound insulation
Where the garage is semi-detached (i.e. next door's garage is on the other side of the wall), sound insulation should be provided to the party wall. This could comprise sound absorbent mineral wool quilt and 2 layers of plasterboard fixed to an independent stud wall with a minimum cavity of 10mm. A skim plaster finish will achieve the necessary fire resistance.

* Floors
Garages normally have a very basic concrete floor slab, about 100mm lower than the floor in the house. Although these sometimes slope down slightly to the front, most are level with the ground

outside, so any rainwater entering under the garage door will find little resistance. The floor will therefore need to be raised to match that of the main house. There are 2 main ways of raising a garage floor:-

Concrete
First the old garage floor slab is levelled with dried sand and a polythene membrane (DPM) is laid over it and lapped up at the edges so it can be tucked into the damp proof course (DPC) in the walls. Then rigid insulation boards placed on top, with the joints between boards taped. These are covered in turn by a second polythene membrane before being levelled up to the same floor height as the house by spreading a concrete or cement screed on top. The screed is minimum 65mm thick and reinforced with an anti-crack mesh.

Timber
Having laid a polythene sheet DPM over the old floor slab (first levelling the floor with sand), treated timber joists can be positioned on top with insulation squashed between the joists.
Floor boards or a deck of T&G chipboard panels can then be screwed in place on top.
Alternatively, a new 'floating floor' can be constructed. Having first covered the garage floor with a DPM as described above, polyurethane insulation boards are laid on top – a 100mm thickness should easily meet the heat loss U-value standard of 0.22 W/m2K (polyurethane provides better performance than traditional polystyrene /styrofoam boards). A vapour barrier membrane sheet is then laid above the insulation before installing the new floor surface, such as T&G wooden floorboards. Laminate or wood floor coverings are a popular choice of finish.

However before deciding which type of floor structure to use, bear in mind that this can be a good opportunity to fit underfloor heating, saving space by dispensing with bulky radiators.
Also, it's worth noting that in areas where naturally occurring radon gas is present in the ground, a radon sump can be provided near the new front wall, connecting the hardcore under the concrete floor with a pipe directed to the outside. Any such requirements can be checked in advance with local authority Building Control.

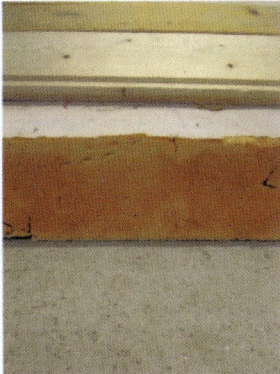

* Roofs
Flat roofs to garages are notoriously basic, and often need to be rebuilt, at least in part. The joists are usually OK but old chipboard decks will need replacing, as will any deck where damp has penetrated. At the very least, the roof will need insulating to achieve the permitted heat loss U value of 0.21 W/m2K (for pitched roofs it's a more demanding 0.16 W/m2K). A layer of thick insulation boards placed on top of the deck with a triple covering of good quality mineral felt above should achieve this. Alternatively 270mm of mineral wool can be placed between the joists (above the ceiling) with 50mm ventilation space above (and vents to fascias).

For pitched roofs, you will need to fit a new plasterboard ceiling with 300mm loft insulation laid on top, and the loft space ventilated in the same way as conventional lofts (e.g. via vents to eaves, tiles or gables). This project is explained in detail in the next chapter, as well as in our sister guide '*Home Renovation On A Budget*' in this series.

* Garage doors
Perhaps the biggest design issue is how best to fill the gaping hole left by the old garage door. With integral or attached garages this will clearly have a major impact on your the appearance of your home, so an obviously cheap infill will risk spoiling the look of the entire house. It needs to be done in sympathy with the rest of the property, to look like it's always been there. Selecting a suitable new front window is obviously crucial, but it doesn't have to be fitted until later in the job to provide access for the works. The old door opening generally needs to be narrowed a bit on either side as a full width window can appear out of proportion.

Perhaps the biggest challenge is matching the new masonry in with the existing on the front elevation. Getting a really good brick match can be difficult, so some firms offer a brick tinting service. Other design options include timber cladding, which can provide a 'barn style' alternative, tile hanging, or decorative render. You could even install a lightweight timber framed panel with thick rigid insulation boards applied internally – which would be easier to remove if you, or a future owner, ever wanted to reinstate the garage.

If you're converting a detached garage it can be a great opportunity to make a big design statement with a fully glazed front gable. Similarly, where the side wall of the garage adjoins your garden, installing glass doors can add an appealing 'studio' flavour. But from a technical viewpoint, highly glazed walls mean increased heat loss – which will need to be counterbalanced with higher insulation levels elsewhere.

Supporting the new wall
It may be only an 'infill' job at the front but Building Control will want to see proper support to the new front (or rear) wall. This could take the form of a pair of 100 x 150mm deep concrete lintels (or 100 x 140 pre-stressed lintels) spanning the opening of a single garage door (one for each leaf of the new wall). The lintel ends need to be cut into the existing brickwork at least 150mm on each side.
In some cases there may be an existing foundation running under the door opening that can be used to support the new wall – the only way to tell is by digging a hole to find out!

Where a new foundation needs to be excavated it will normally need to be at least 500mm below finished ground level (or possibly deeper depending on ground conditions). The new wall will also require a DPC, cavity insulation and dry-lining internally to boost thermal efficiency, as for a new extension. However where you opt for a lightweight timber frame infill wall (plus window) a more limited form of support may be acceptable.

* Windows, light and ventilation
Normally a single new window to the front or back will provide all the light you need. But the planners may not accept new side windows within 2.4m of a boundary, in order to respect neighbours' privacy (but then you probably won't need to make a planning application!).

From a design perspective, it's important that new windows on main elevations are aligned with the existing windows at their tops, not at the sills – it just looks better that way! (when converting integral or attached garages). In garages with roofs (i.e. not integral garages) installing a skylight or 'light tube' on top can work wonders in boosting daylight.

In terms of performance, windows must achieve a 'U-value' heat loss target no greater than 1.6W/m2K (or have at least a 'C' Window Energy Rating - WER). To meet this requirement will mean specifying reasonably high performance double glazed units. Openings for windows and doors formed in cavity walls should have standard cavity closers fitted, which can double as a DPC around the frame whilst insulating the reveals to prevent 'cold bridging'. Windows should also have an openable area equal to 1/20th of the floor area of the room to provide 'rapid ventilation'. In addition, background trickle vents are required (which should come ready-fitted to new door and window frames).

New kitchens, bathrooms, utilities and cloakroom/WCs will need extractor fans, and living rooms with fires and fuel burning appliances may require additional air vents in walls.

Where the new room can't be accessed directly via a door from a hallway (so it's accessed via another room) then it will need a safe and easy exit route in the event of fire. Most windows can provide suitable 'means of escape' as long as they have an opening casement or sash large enough to allow you to escape if you were trapped in the room by a fire. This means they need an unobstructed opening area of at least 0.33 sq m and a minimum width and height of 450mm, with a maximum floor to sill height of 1100 mm.

* Services
Garages often contain inconveniently positioned gas/electric meters and consumer units. The simplest solution is to neatly box in the cables and pipes, since moving them can be expensive. The cost of having an electric meter and all the associated wiring moved can easily exceed £1000. In some houses the boiler is located in the garage. Modern 'room-sealed ' appliances have balanced flues projecting through the main wall, so it should be possible to enclose boilers within a new cupboard. But when it comes to running new electrics, Part P of the Building Regulations restricts the amount you can do yourself, so this is best left to the professionals. Electricians can normally self-certify their installations if they're registered with a body that gives them the necessary 'registered installer' status. Upon completion of the job, it is a legal requirement for the electrician to test the new system and hand over a signed electrical safety certificate.

Extending the central heating to add an extra radiator or two can be done on a DIY basis, but if the old system is getting on a bit and can't cope with the extra load you may be in for some extra expense upgrading or replacing it. Note that all work involving gas fittings and appliances must by law be carried out by Gas Safe registered heating engineers.

* Kitchens & bathrooms
If you want a new kitchen, bathroom or continental-style wet room, the plumbing logistics will need to be planned in advance. But the feasibility of plumbing in new kitchens and bathrooms will depend on the position of your existing drains. When planning your layouts, make sure there are sufficient routes for both waste and supply pipes. The waste from any new appliances, sinks and baths etc will need to connect to the existing foul drainage system as they are not allowed to be connected into rainwater drains. So your options may be constrained by the layout of the house. Note that extractor fans will also be required in new kitchens, bathrooms, utilities and cloakrooms.

* New door openings
With integral and attached garages, there may already be a doorway leading from the house directly into the garage, which will normally be fitted with a self-closing fire door (because of the potential risk of fires from vehicles). If not, then a new opening can be cut through the wall. But first take expert advice as it may well be a load-bearing wall.

5.
Converting Outbuildings
extra space you didn't know you had !

Turning a redundant outbuilding into a new home office or studio can be a great way to add extra space on a budget. Reincarnated as an annexe it could instead provide private accommodation for guests, elderly parents, or twentysomething offspring who are still living at home but need some independence.

Many properties have outbuildings in the garden that are under-used, such as old 'brick privies' or summerhouses, usually languishing in an unloved state crammed with junk. Former Council houses are particularly well endowed with attached stores. Farmhouses and properties with large grounds may have disused stable blocks or barns. Either way, there is often potential to convert such buildings at minimal cost to provide new useable space.

In practical terms, the work required to upgrade outbuildings is essential the same as outlined in the previous chapter for garage conversions, so you might want to flip back a few pages for more detailed advice. However, the main problem with outbuildings is that they're often in very poor condition and may need fairly extensive renovation before they can be usefully converted. Renovation works are covered in our sister guide *'Home Renovation On A Budget'*.

So the first task is to assess condition of the existing structure. Typically these are very basic single storey buildings with walls of thin 105mm single skin brick or blockwork with no DPC. So check for stability and defects. Timber outbuildings such as summerhouses will often be even more basic, but can be upgraded as long as they are free from rot and are structurally stable.

QUESTIONS TO ASK UP FRONT

* Can you convert without planning permission? In most cases the answer is 'yes' – see Permitted Development Rights below. However you will still need to make a Building Regulations application.

* What sort of buildings are suitable? Where outbuildings are in very poor condition the best option is normally to demolish and rebuild. It's often possible for old bricks and roof tiles etc to be salvaged and re-used, saving money. It may also be worth considering rebuilding it on a larger scale, in which case you might want to skip forward to the next chapter which looks at the rules concerning the construction of new garden buildings.

* Will it add value?
Generally the answer is yes. Unlike garage conversions you're not likely to be sacrificing anything particularly useful to create your new space. However the amount it adds value will depend on how useful the new space is to a buyer. Well converted 'home offices' are particularly popular features.

What will it cost?
This is one of the cheaper ways of adding space - but much will depend on what state the building is in. Having to rebuild the roof for example will obviously add to the expense. But generally speaking costs are broadly similar to those garage conversions (see previous chapter). One of the attractions of this sort of project is that much of the remodelling work can often be undertaken on a DIY basis. It helps for example that these buildings are usually single storey so there's no need for scaffolding. And by doing some of the work yourself it should be possible to do the job for less half the cost of employing builders.

If however you do decide to employ builders, the quoted price should include all the necessary drawings and fees for local authority consents, and a Building Control completion certificate must be provided at the end of the job. Before proceeding, think carefully about exactly what you want, including the position of all the sockets and radiators, as changing your mind later can be expensive. Alternatively, if you want to manage the job yourself a local architect can be employed to produce drawings and a specification for the Building Control application.

Minimising disturbance
So that home life can carry on as normal it pays to plan the following aspects in advance.

* Access for builders should be planned early on to minimise disruption (e.g. via a side gate to the garden).

* Deliveries: So that building materials can be delivered and safely stored it's a good idea to allocate space .

* Services: The existing electrical systems will normally need to be extended for lighting and power circuits. So schedule a day for this work when the main supply can be temporarily cut off without causing too much disruption.

PLANNING & BUILDING REGS

You do not normally need planning permission to convert an attached outbuilding (such as an adjoining store) into living accommodation. Indeed any outbuilding, even those located some way down the garden, should be acceptable for conversion under 'Permitted Development Rights' assuming it will be used for normal residential activities associated with the main house.

The key question is 'what's the intended use?' And the basic rule with outbuildings is that the proposed new use must be 'ancillary to the use and enjoyment of your home as a single dwelling'. This means you're not allowed to *build new* sleeping accommodation such as a 'granny flat' or annexe in the garden – because that would be tantamount to building a separate dwelling.

However, you are allowed to *convert existing* outbuildings into new sleeping accommodation provided it's used as part of your home. This shouldn't require planning permission but conversions to 'self-contained annexes' can be contentious. As a rule however, creating an annexe will be acceptable as long as the use is 'incidental to the enjoyment of the dwelling house'. This means it can be used as a home as long as it is only occupied by guests or members of the main household. It cannot be let to anyone else without first getting planning permission for 'independent use'. Planners are often reluctant to grant permission for independent use, as the building could later be sold off separately from the main house and potentially be replaced by a new, larger dwelling. So features like separate external access and stairs may not be accepted because they could facilitate future use as a separate dwelling.

This may sound unnecessarily restrictive but if there wasn't a limit on new dwellings most gardens would by now have been sub-divided into multiple building plots.

Permitted Development Rights also cover demolition, so long as the building to be demolished is no larger than 50 m2 total area, measured externally (including the walls). You should also be able to enlarge existing outbuildings, as describe in the next chapter.

As always, it's important to remember that Permitted Development Rights may not apply for some properties, in which case a planning application will be required - so always check with your local Planning Authority at the design stage. For example restrictions apply for Listed buildings. However being located in a Conservation Area shouldn't normally pose any significant restrictions because outbuildings tend to be single storey and usually sited well away from the front of the house.

Building Regulations
If an outbuilding is to be used as a habitable room then it must be upgraded to meet the Building Regulations requirements for 'a material change of use'. You will therefore need to make an application to Building Control. There are a number of areas where your conversion will need to comply, as outlined in the previous chapter. Briefly, the structure will need to be insulated, while windows will need to be replaced with double glazed units. All new heating, electrics and plumbing will also need to comply.

The necessary works to upgrade and remodel outbuildings are largely the same as those described in the previous chapter. But there are some additional issues that may also need to be addressed:-

* Removing asbestos

A lot of older outbuildings and some garages contain asbestos cement sheeting, which was widely used as a durable, rigid, flat roof covering (usually corrugated), and sometimes for walls panels. It also crops up in the form of gutters, downpipes, flues, water tanks and even in some textured paints. White asbestos (chrysotile) was still used until finally banned in November 1999.This isn't necessarily a problem as long as you don't disturb the material by sanding or drilling, releasing dangerous fibres that could be inhaled. If the material needs to be removed it can be done without a licence or employing a specialist firm, although care must be taken to minimise any fibre release. So wearing a mask is a wise precaution when working with these materials.

Note that asbestos cement is a fragile material and is not weight bearing never venture on top of it without crawling boards. To minimise any risk of releasing fibres avoid breaking the sheets - try to remove them whole – and dampen them as a precaution before working. Above all don't use power tools.

In many cases the bolts or screws securing the sheeting can be loosened without too much trouble and the material safely removed. Otherwise the most practical solution is to conceal asbestos cement sheeting behind new coverings, e.g. by lining it internally with plasterboard (fixed to new timber studwork) or externally with a suitable cladding such as weatherboarding. Roofs of this type are best rebuilt, or if if all else fails it can be clad-over with new sheeting material.

When it comes to disposal, householders are normally allowed to take small amounts, say 4 or 5 sheets, to local Household Waste Recycling Centres ('the Council Tips'), but rules can vary locally. Where licensed contactors are employed they are likely to charge a premium despite the associated risks normally being very small. They will need to take the material to a site licensed for the disposal of hazardous waste.

* Extending the electrics
The existing electrical system will need to be extended to provide new lighting and socket outlets. Most electrical work is restricted under Part P of the Building Regulations, including supplies to gardens and outbuildings such as sheds, garages and greenhouses, even garden pond pumps. New installations serving outbuildings must be done professionally as botched external DIY cable runs are a common cause of electrocution. New external supplies should have their own consumer unit with RCD protection. Supply cables to detached outbuildings sited away from the house must be run in armoured cable and fully protected.
Electricians can normally self-certify their installations if they're registered with a body that gives them the necessary 'registered installer' status. Upon completion of the job, it is a legal requirement for the electrician to test the new system and hand over a signed electrical safety certificate.

* New service connections
Attached outbuildings can normally utilise the water, gas and electric supplies from the house. Existing central heating systems can also usually be extended without too much trouble. However 'stand alone' outbuildings located further down the garden will need new water and electric supplies, and possibly also drainage. Phone cables are rarely needed thanks to the use of mobiles, and cordless phones which can transmit signals up to about a 10 metre range.

Water connections should have a subsidiary stopcock in the house and also to the outbuilding so the supply can be cut if necessary without affecting domestic use. New polyethylene water supply pipes can be laid in a service trench bedded in gravel and protected from frost with lagging on entry/exit points and within the new outbuilding.

Any new sewer connections must comply with Building Regs and the utility company should also be notified. A well insulated outbuilding should require very little in the way of heating, so a small electric heater may be sufficient. Larger annexes may want their own independent heating system (e.g. LPG gas or via an oil supply) serving either a small combination boiler, or a small electric water heater, depending on demand. Note that gas supplies can only be altered or installed by Gas Safe Registered engineers.

* Floors
In most cases foundations are likely to be minimal or non-existent, and buildings may instead be built on a simple concrete slab. But this needn't be a problem; many period cottages have little in the way of 'footings' and have survived perfectly happily for centuries. However a lack of foundations means that seasonal ground movement will be transmitted to the outbuilding which therefore needs to be able to accommodate a small amount of 'shuffling about' without cracking. So when repairing old masonry walls, flexible traditional materials like lime based mortars, renders and plasters should be used.

In some cases the outbuilding will simply be sitting on chunky timber or concrete bearers, in turn resting on a concrete slab. As long as they're in sound condition this can be acceptable. But the floor will need insulating from the cold. The finished floor surface should be at least 150mm above ground level and there should be a thick plastic DPC under the lowest timbers to prevent damp rising up from the ground, plus a good flow of air under the deck. Otherwise demolition and rebuilding may be a better option.

In most outbuildings built with traditional brick or stone walls, the floor will be very rudimentary and not much higher than the ground outside. So to prevent damp and ingress of surface water from the garden the floor will normally need to be built up to about 200mm above ground level (as described earlier for garages). Raised door thresholds can also help keep damp at bay.

* Walls
As with most garages, the walls will normally be relatively thin (e.g. single brick) and will need lining on the inside. Fortunately the roof loadings are taken by the existing walls, so the purpose of building a new inner leaf is primarily to to make the building thermally efficient, and less vulnerable to condensation forming on cold walls. There are 3 main options and both are likely to shrink useable width of room by about 100 -150mm.

Option1: The simplest method of upgrading existing walls is to construct a new studwork inner leaf built off 2 courses of engineering bricks, leaving a 50mm cavity. This framework is then packed with insulation boards (e.g. polyurethane) or mineral wool batts. It can then be lined internally with an additional layer of insulation boards or with foil-backed insulated plasterboard over a vapour barrier sheet. A skim plaster or direct decoration finish can then be applied.

Option 2: A new internal leaf can be built from lightweight *thermalite* blocks (non-load-bearing) which have reasonable insulation properties. This can be lined internally with insulated plasterboard for improved insulation or plastered and decorated.

Option 3: The most effective method of insulating walls is to line them externally with rigid sheets of insulation, typically 100mm thick. Materials such as polyurethane or natural woodfibre boards are ideal and can be secured to the walls using special plastic fixings and adhesives, supported at the base on metal rails. The insulation can then be given an exterior finish such as render (cement or traditional lime) or timber weatherboarding. The main challenge is having to remove and re-instate any downpipes etc, and to extend the roof coverings at the eaves above.

* Roofs
As with garages, most outbuilding roofs are extremely basic, typically just simple flat roofs (see 'asbestos' above). If you're lucky there may be a pitched tiled roof.

Pitched roofs
These are often in need of a general overhaul – replacing any slipped or missing tiles. Where slopes have bowed they may need beefing up with extra rafters or support from a new purlin timber run across the underside of the rafters. All structural work must be done in accordance with Building Regs.

But being relatively small, single storey buildings, where significant attention is required roofs can be stripped by lifting off the tiles and removing old battens to expose the timber structure. This can then be treated for any active beetle or rot, with any decay or weakened timbers cut out and replaced. If necessary, the structure can be strengthened and a breather membrane laid over the rafters before re-battening. Where you have a conventional loft with a ceiling, this can be insulated with mineral wool quilt.

However this is a good opportunity to insulate the roof above the rafters (a warm roof'). Being insulated from above, this gives you the option of leaving the roof structure exposed as a feature. This is done by first nailing sheets of plywood or OSB over the rafter which will help strengthen the roof structure. Next, rigid insulation boards (e.g. 50mm Kingspan polyurethane) are laid on top of the freshly boarded rafters. These are held in place by counter-battening – fixing 'vertical' battens to the outer face of the insulation down the line of each rafter using helical fixings, nails or dry wall screws into the plywood boards or rafters underneath. Finally sheets of breather membrane underlay are spread on top of the counter-battens, held in place by conventional new horizontal battens from which the tiles are hung. Unless damaged, the original tiles can normally be re-used.

Flat roofs
Flat roofs are generally built like timber floors – from '4 x 2'in (100 x 50mm) joists clad with some form of boarding (e.g. softwood floorboards or plywood). The main difference is the provision of tapered

'firings' above the joists to provide a shallow slope of about 5 to 10 degrees, plus of course a surface covering. Less common are longer lasting reinforced concrete roofs usually with some form of bitumen/asphalt surface.

On timber flat roofs, mineral felt is the most widely used covering material on account of its relatively low cost and ease of installation. It is made from bitumen-coated fabric, usually laid in 3 layers bedded in hot bitumen. But with a lifespan of only 10 to 15 years re-covering may now be overdue (although longevity is improved by solar reflective coatings such as stone chippings). Of course roofs don't have to be re-covered in relatively short-life felt. But the cost of fitting high quality lead sheet can make it uneconomic. Other materials with superior performance to roofing felts, could be considered, such as fibreglass and EPDM synthetic rubber.

* Insulation
To comply with Part L of the Building Regs, the roof will need to be fully insulated to current standards. To achieve the target U-value of 0.18Wm2/K or better, a 100mm depth of polyurethane boarding laid on top of the deck should be sufficient. But this may not always be feasible and there are other options:-

a/ Above the decking ('*warm deck'*)

Laying thick high performance insulation boards on top of the existing deck should transform it into a snug new 'warm roof' that's inherently immune to condensation. In most cases this is the best option, the main constraint being whether raising the height of the roof by up to 150mm is likely to present any problems. For example if there's a very low window on an adjacent wall, it could make the detailing tricky (e.g. at upstands tucked into mortar joints). The guttering and fascias are also are likely to need modification.

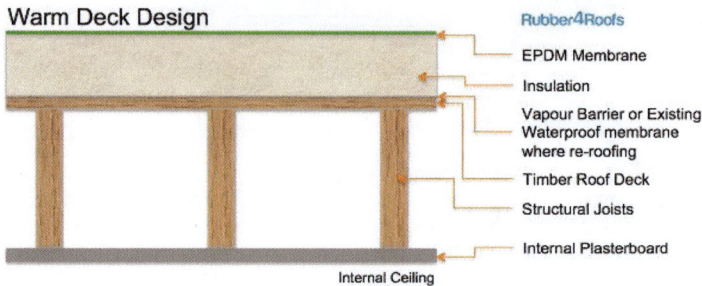

Warm Deck Design

Rubber4Roofs

- EPDM Membrane
- Insulation
- Vapour Barrier or Existing Waterproof membrane where re-roofing
- Timber Roof Deck
- Structural Joists
- Internal Plasterboard

Internal Ceiling

Once the old roof covering has been stripped, the condition of the deck must be checked. Old chipboard decks are especially prone to developing problems as they have poor water resistance. If the deck shows signs of rot or damage, it should be replaced with a new layer of 18mm marine plywood or OSB, and the insulation boards laid on top prior to re-felting.

b/ Below the ceiling ('cold deck')

Unless the roof covering needs replacing anyway, it may be simpler to tackle the job from indoors working from below, retaining the existing 'cold deck' arrangement. There are 2 main ways you can insulate from below:-

* Keep the existing ceiling in place and fix a new layer of thick rigid insulated plasterboard directly onto the existing ceiling. First apply a vapour control sheet so it's sandwiched above the new layer to keep moisture at bay. A thickness of at least 50mm should be achievable.

* Again keeping the existing ceiling in place, a new suspended ceiling can be constructed underneath the old one – subject to available headroom. A new false ceiling can be built using fairly shallow joists (100mm x 50mm depending on the span). A gap of at least 50mm can be left so the new structure 'floats' independently of the old ceiling. The void can then be packed with mineral wool quilt. Again, a vapour control sheet should first be applied to prevent moist air getting into the structure.

c/ Above the ceiling   (*also 'cold deck'*)

It's possible to do things the old fashioned way by 'filling the void' between the existing joists, as long as you leave a 50mm ventilation path on top of the insulation with air vents to the fascias. Maintaining an air flow is important to help disperse any humid air that gets in from the rooms below before it gets a chance to condense and make the roof and ceiling damp. So with typical 200mm deep joists you should be able to squeeze up to 150mm depth of insulation above the ceiling.

Cold Deck Design

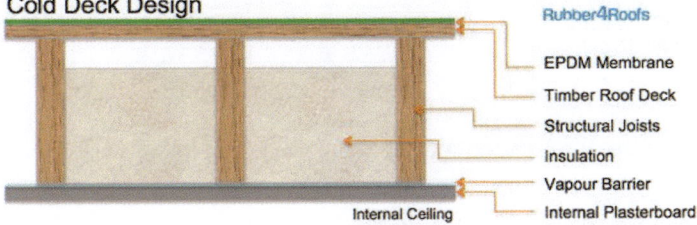

Rubber4Roofs

- EPDM Membrane
- Timber Roof Deck
- Structural Joists
- Insulation
- Vapour Barrier
- Internal Plasterboard

Internal Ceiling

If you don't mind the enormous amount of dust and mess access can be gained by tearing down and replacing the existing ceiling. Once the joists are exposed, thick rolls of wool or semi-rigid wool batts (or rigid boards cut to shape) can be placed between them, taking care to leave the necessary air gap on top. A new ceiling can then be installed with sheets of plasterboard fixed to the undersides of the joists over a vapour control sheet.

Alternatively, to save all the trouble and mess of taking down the ceiling, adding the insulation is often easier from above (where access is possible). But clearly this will require the temporary removal of the roof covering and deck – so this is a job that's best combined with renewal works when the coverings need replacing anyway.

6.
Garden Buildings

Why go to all the trouble of extending or converting when you can simply order a new, ready-made 'studio' or 'garden office' and have it delivered and erected in a day? Probably the easiest way to add more space is to buy one 'fresh out of the box' – factory insulated with integral electrics and IT communications. Alternatively there's nothing to stop you designing bespoke new accommodation perfectly tailored to your needs, and building it from scratch. Playrooms, hobby rooms, offices, studios, rehearsal rooms, games rooms – in fact just about any use can be accommodated, either by building from scratch, or ordering a factory-constructed 'pod', 'studio' or 'lodge'.

Unsurprisingly, suppliers of garden buildings claim that they offer significantly better value than the equivalent extension. On balance, the all-inclusive price per square metre is probably not much less than the cost of constructing a simple extension, but it should be less hassle and quicker to arrange. Although it should also add value to your property, because garden buildings don't directly enlarge the floor area of the house, the increase is likely to be less than for the equivalent extension.

There is of course one very important question to resolve before getting too carried away. What legal restrictions are there when it comes to erecting new buildings in gardens? Let's be honest, nothing causes more anguish between neighbours than when a large new structure suddenly appears in next door's garden, glowering menacingly over the fence and potentially ruining your view. So before embarking on a similar course of action it's important to know precisely where you stand with regard to your planning rights.

QUESTIONS TO ASK UP FRONT

* Can it be done without planning permission? In most cases the answer is 'yes' – see Permitted Development Rights below. However you may still need to make a Building Regulations application.

* What's included in package for a ready-made 'garden office'? You may still need to provide service connections (at least electrical connections) and a concrete slab base. But do they charge extra for delivery and erection on site?

* What will it cost? Both options - constructing a brand new garden building, or ordering one ready-made - are relatively easy to price, without the 'unknowns' that can bedevil conversion projects. Whilst not the cheapest methods of adding space, there are a number of ways you can keep the price down, discussed below.

For ready made garden buildings prices can be checked online, but typical costs are likely to be in the region of £10k – 15k. Small 'micropods' may be cheaper, and larger 'garden lodges' and insulated garden studios can cost as much as £35,000.

* What about Council Tax? Building a separate annexe equipped as a self-contained 'granny flat' means it will be registered separately for Council Tax. The tax is typically levied at the lowest band and is payable even when the building is empty (although there's a 50 per cent reduction for the first 6 months after it becomes unoccupied). To get the liability lifted you'd need to remove either the kitchen or the bathroom together with the associated plumbing, to demonstrate that it's not fully self-contained.

Minimising disturbance
* Access to the garden needs to be considered in advance to minimise disruption. If you're ordering a 'garden office' this will probably be delivered in kit form and erected on site, so check the largest size components in advance.

* Deliveries: So that building materials such as sand, bricks and timber can be delivered and safely stored it's best to allocate space in advance.

* Services: The existing electrical systems will normally need to be extended. So schedule a day for this work when the main supply can be temporarily cut off without causing too much disruption.

PLANNING & BUILDING REGS

It is not always appreciated that you can normally erect new outbuildings, such as garden offices,
garages, summerhouses and sheds, without the need for planning consent. Inevitably however the
Permitted Development Rights (PDRs) that make this libertarian paradise possible are subject to a
number of limitations – see the rules listed below. The bottom line is that there is considerable scope
to build new outbuildings covering up to half of your garden, up to four metres in height. But
outbuildings that do not meet the rules, and do not have planning permission, will be in breach of
planning law so enforcement action can be taken:-

* Location: The outbuilding must not be built forward of the front (or principle) elevation, and should
not be visible from the road

* Height: Must be single storey. Buildings with conventional pitched roofs have a maximum height limit
of 4 metres and the eaves no higher than 2.5 metres. For flat roofs the limit is 3 metres (and the same
for mono-pitched roofs).

* Height near boundaries: Where outbuildings are sited closer than 2 metres to a boundary the
maximum height is reduced to 2.5 metres.

* New outbuildings must be 'for the use and enjoyment of your property', i.e. not a separate dwelling.

* Density: it must not cover more than 50% of the original garden. That means half the total area of
your overall plot within the boundaries – excluding the bit occupied by the original house. But anything
else subsequently built, such as garages, extensions and sheds must be counted as part of the 50%
allowance. Otherwise there are no size limits on the footprint, and no limit on how far away from the
house down the garden you can build.

BUT...

As always it's important to note that PDRs don't apply universally, in which case a planning
application will be required - so always check with your local Planning Authority at the design stage.
There are plenty of modern houses that have had these rights removed. And of course Listed
buildings and those in Conservation Areas are special cases.

Sleeping accommodation

To count as Permitted Development, outbuildings must be used in connection with your home. You're not allowed to build new self-contained sleeping accommodation such as a 'granny flat' in the garden (as it would count as a separate dwelling).

But as we saw in the last chapter, you *are* allowed to convert existing outbuildings for use as sleeping accommodation (subject to Building Regulations). So suppose you decide to built a new gym that happens to have a kitchenette and WC/shower facilities. There is an argument supporting the view that once it's established as an 'existing outbuilding' you should have the right to convert its use to sleeping accommodation. But the question is, how long would it take for it to be recognised as an 'established building'? Possibly 4 years in line with the 4 year rule (see Introduction). But this is unclear and likely to vary depending on the Local Planning Authority.

Of course there's nothing to stop you applying for planning consent to build a new annexe with self-contained sleeping accommodation. But before doing so it would make sense to sound out the Planners as to whether this sort of application is likely to be acceptable. Where the mood militates against such uses, some experts suggest that you might be better off writing down a less contentious use on the application form (such as a playroom), and then a number of years after the building is completed you could apply to change its use.

Building Regulations

When it comes to new outbuildings there are a number of exemptions where the Building Regs will not apply. As you might expect, garden sheds, summerhouses, greenhouses and suchlike aren't covered (defined as 'small detached buildings up to 15 sq metres floor area containing no sleeping accommodation').

The Building Regulations may also not apply for buildings with a larger floor area of between 15 and 30 sq metres, providing they contain no sleeping accommodation AND are located at least 1 metre from any boundary or where the building is constructed of non-combustible materials. So for example a new detached double garage would be OK. As a general rule, if a building is not for habitable use, it won't be of interest to Building Control. But the rules can be difficult to interpret, so for our purposes – adding extra space - it's best to assume that compliance is required. After all the whole point of compliance is to end up with a safe structurally sound, warm and well insulated building. And when one day you come to sell your house, the buyers solicitors will ask for a copy of the Building Regs completion certificate to prove that your new accommodation was properly built.

There are a number of areas where new accommodation will need to comply with the Building Regs. These are basically the same the ones described in previous chapters on garage conversions and home extensions.

DESIGN MATTERS

* Maximising useable space
Although new outbuildings are limited to 4 metres in height, you could always excavate a little deeper to form a 'semi-basement' ground floor, so the roof space could be sufficiently large for use as accommodation.

* Floors
There are three possible types of ground floor construction: solid concrete, suspended concrete and suspended timber. Most outbuildings, being relatively small, are likely to be of traditional solid concrete. Floors in larger buildings are generally better suited to the standard method used in new home construction, 'beam & block' suspended concrete. As well as supporting the room's contents, occupants and its own weight ground floors need to provide resistance to moisture and prevent heat loss.

* Extending the services

The existing electrical system will need to be extended to provide lighting and power socket outlets. You may also need water and drainage, or even gas or oil for heating – as described in the previous chapter for converting outbuildings.

* Foundations

Excavating foundations for new buildings can raise a number of potential issues. Where these are a concern it might be better to to opt for a ready-made 'garden office' which can be placed on on a simple a concrete slab, rather than having to excavate deep trench foundations.

Adjacent structures

It is important to ensure that excavation for new foundations does not undermine nearby buildings Where your new trench runs close to and alongside another building, it's a good idea to excavate only short lengths at a time, and then concrete each part of the new foundation in turn to avoid undermining a whole length of an adjacent structure. You will also need to comply with the Party Wall Act.

Drains and sewers

The loads from a building are transferred down via the foundations to the ground, spreading down and outwards at an angle of about 45 degrees. If there's a drain or sewer is within this area, it could be damaged and possibly crack. To prevent this, new foundations should normally be built at least at least as deep as the sewer. But in the first instance contact the local drainage authority responsible for the sewer to check whether any legal agreement is required.

Trees

The presence of nearby trees, especially in areas with clay soils, means your new foundations will need to be significantly deeper. Building Control will need to approve foundation depths.

7.
Opening Up Usable Space
Transforming your home's layout

When you think about it, the obvious way to boost your living space is by making the most of the accommodation you've already got. In many homes the internal layout is inefficiently arranged, so remodelling it to suit today's lifestyles can work wonders. This approach also has the advantage of being a relatively inexpensive way of gaining extra space in your home.

Improving the layout might involve something as simple as building a new stud partition wall to divide a very large bedroom, or adding a first floor bathroom. Conversely, it might involve taking down internal walls to create a bright open plan kitchen/diner. Sometimes more complex projects like re-locating the stairs or removing chimney breasts are undertaken, although these are major works and rarely succeed in freeing up much extra space.

QUESTIONS TO ASK UP FRONT

Before starting some key points need to be checked:-

* Can walls be knocked down, or new ones built, without planning permission? In most cases the answer is 'yes' – see Permitted Development Rights below. However you may still need to make a Building Regulations application.

* Is my house suitable? Some houses offer more potential space gains than others – those with lots of small, pokey rooms or dark and dingy inner lobbies can often benefit from 'opening up'. Those with overly-large rooms may have potential to subdivide. It also helps if you don't have too many obstacles that need moving, like wall mounted boilers, cupboards, pipework and electric switches and sockets.

* What will it cost? This should be relatively inexpensive. Constructing a new studwork partition wall is a fairly straightforward DIY project. Taking out internal load-bearing walls is more complex, but nothing a good builder couldn't do in a day, the main cost being labour. Money can be saved where you undertake some of the finishing work and decoration yourself.

* Will it add to the value of my home? Often the answer will be no – where the changes are primarily designed to suit your personal lifestyle, such as dividing up a bedroom. It helps if these sort of alterations are 'reversible', so a future buyer could re-instate the original layout. In period properties removing original features like chimney breasts and stairs is not advisable, as it can actually detract from the appeal and hence reduce the home's value. Taking out walls to entrance halls can also detract from period charm, and is not advisable where the loft has potential for conversion, as separate hallways are important when it comes to complying with Fire Regulations. On the other hand creating a spacious open-plan kitchen/diner can be a very appealing feature, boosting a property's desirability and value.

Adding an extra bedroom should in theory add value – because estate agents routinely describe properties by the number of bedrooms – but not if the job's badly done or the rooms are small, dark and pokey.

PLANNING & BUILDING REGS

Changing internal layouts is not something that will normally be of much interest to the Planners. The main exception is of course with Listed buildings where consent is always required. There's also the grey area where planning consent was originally granted let's say for a 3 bedroom house, so dividing it up to make a 4 bedder may be stretching what's strictly permissible. This can be more of a concern where you plan to rent out the room, as local authority Environmental Health will want to make sure the property doesn't count as a House In Multiple Occupation (HMO), which may need licensing.

Building Regulations consent is required for all structural alterations. So any taking out of walls, chimney breasts, stairs etc, or even widening an existing opening will require notification to Building Control and an application to be made. Any new bedrooms created will need to comply in terms of natural light from windows and ventilation, and possibly fire safety.

Changing the layout
Changing the internal layout of a property can be one of the best ways of transforming its appeal without spending a fortune. If the 'flow' of your home isn't quite right, it may be possible to create a more contemporary environment and better use of space by opening up the hallway, removing doorways or repositioning internal walls.

Carefully planned, layout alterations can be highly successful at overcoming drawbacks with the original design. For example houses with a warren of small, dark rooms can benefit enormously from the improved light gained by opening-up. And in many older homes the kitchens are relatively small, so taking out the wall separating the kitchen and adjoining dining room can dramatically improved the layout at minimal cost compared to building a new extension.

Taking out internal walls to open up the living space can be very tempting especially in smaller dwellings, for example 'knocking through' front and rear reception rooms. But in some cases this can be structurally unwise because 'spine walls' play a crucial role in supporting loadings from the roof and upper floors. And in period buildings there's a danger of creating a sterile environment devoid of the historic features and original layouts that many buyers demand, thereby reducing the value of the property. It's also worth bearing in mind that internal partitions can perform a useful function in keep conflicting activities in the home separated. The downside of having a spacious open-plan kitchen/diner is that all your old dishes and clutter are permanently on display.

Removing Internal Walls

Internal walls perform a number of functions. Some are fundamental to the structure of the house, some offer fire protection to the stairway, and others simply divide up the space within the house and are relatively straightforward to alter or remove.

Load-bearing walls are fundamental to the structure of the building and careful consideration needs to be given before they can be altered or removed – work which requires Building Regulations consent. In most cases you will need to consult a Structural Engineer to design the alteration – taking into account the loads supported. They will design a suitable beam or some other supporting structure so the loads carried are safely transmitted to the ground.

Before demolishing an internal wall there are 2 key questions to ask:

Is it load-bearing?

It's not always obvious which walls are holding things up, and which are merely partition walls. But if you get this wrong, you're in serious trouble. In most properties, especially older buildings, the internal walls will normally be supporting roof loadings, floor joists or walls upstairs (see below).

Does it protect you from fire?

Walls around staircases offer protection allowing you to escape in the event of a house fire. Altering these will require Building Regulations consent, even if they're not load-bearing.

Similarly, partition walls that separate entrance halls from reception rooms are best left intact where you might want to convert the loft in future, since they form a ready-made fire escape corridor to comply with Building Regulations.

If these walls are removed, it is essential your home is fitted with mains operated smoke detection and that all rooms have windows suitable for fire escape purposes. If you plan to remove such a wall, contact Building Control who can advise whether any additional work is needed.

How can you tell if an internal wall is 'structural' ?

It's a bit of a myth that if you tap a wall and it sounds hollow it's just a studwork partition that can be ripped out willy nilly. The fact is, some stud walls are load-bearing. Conversely, solid masonry internal walls aren't always 'structural' – some were built as simple partition walls. If in doubt the best advice is to consult a Structural Engineer or Building Surveyor.

To see if an internal wall is load bearing, check if it's supporting:-

* Roof Loadings

In older houses the roof structure often relies on support from an internal wall. More modern roofs with 'W' shaped roof trusses (introduced in the late 1960s) are designed to span right across the house from one main wall to another without internal support.

* Floor loadings

Floor joists rarely span more than about 3 or 4 metres without support from an internal wall or beam. The direction of joists is often the shorter span in a room from wall to wall. Look for nail runs in floorboards to see direction of joists (at right angles to direction of floor boards).

* Loadings from walls above

Ground floor walls often continue upstairs as bedroom walls. However sometimes upstairs walls are offset or supported on a beam. Most modern houses have lightweight stud walls upstairs.

* Lateral support

In older houses, internal walls sometimes provide 'lateral support' helping to tie together the adjoining walls either side.

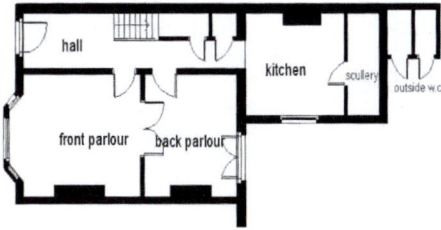

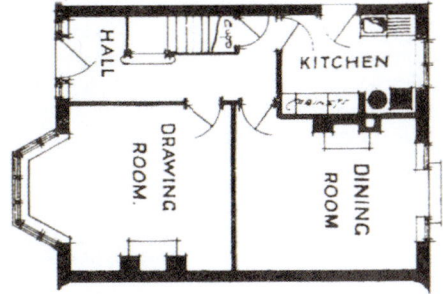

Illustrations LEFT: typical Victorian ground floor layout. RIGHT: typical 1930s ground floor

* Making structural alterations

Before making any sort of structural alteration to your home a Building Regulations application must be made. Building Control will then inspect the work on site as it progresses and ultimately issue a completion certificate to show that it complies with the Building Regulations.

As well as 'knocking through' internal walls there are several other types of popular structural alteration, such as the removal of chimney breasts to free up living space, and enlarging openings in main walls to install wide bi-fold garden doors.

If such works are carried out illegally without consent, it can cause major problems when you come to sell or re-mortgage – as well as being potentially dangerous. So it's worth taking advantage of the service provided by Building Control who will be checking the work and can also offer professional advice.

Design

Before making any structural alteration you obviously need to come up with an alternative means of support. A structural engineer will need to calculate loadings and design a suitable solution. For example, where chimney breasts are removed, the remaining masonry above (to the loft or an upstairs room) will still be taking loadings from the chimney stack and will need to be supported. This normally requires the insertion of a suitable steel beam supported at either end, for example on padstones set into a load-bearing wall.

Similarly, where load-bearing internal walls are taken out, a steel beam will normally need to be inserted to safely transfer the load from the upstairs wall, floors or roof to the side or party walls. But some older party walls can be remarkably weak and weedy, and may not be up to the job of supporting extra loadings. This would require an alternative solution such as new brick piers or steel columns to be built either end of the new beam, which could mean having to excavate small foundations internally, adding to the expense and mess.

Making a new opening

When making structural alterations, some temporary method of support must be provided before any demolition is carried out. For example, when taking out a wall, the masonry above must be supported while a slot is cut for the new lintel. This is done by first cutting holes just above the position of the proposed new lintel through which sturdy timber 'needles' are placed. These are supported on either side by adjustable steel 'acro' props which should rest on a scaffold plank to spread the load.

New lintels should normally extend either side of the proposed opening by at least 150mm bearing. To spread the load, additional support will be needed under the ends of the lintel, such as a padstone or a hard engineering bricks. Once safely supported, the new opening can be cut out underneath.

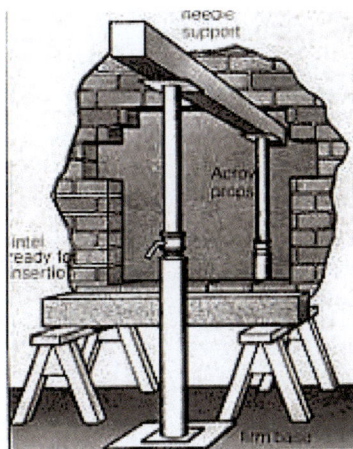

What if illegal structural alterations have already been made to your home?

If structural alterations have been carried out without Building Regs approval, the assumption is they are potentially dangerous. Things like removed chimney breasts or internal walls are sometimes done without permission, and may have been botched before being covered up.

Often it's only when you're moving house that a lack of consent becomes apparent. This can be a deal breaker, causing serious last minute problems and adding to the stress of moving house. Where Building Regulations consent wasn't obtained for structural alterations they may be dangerous. If a Completion Certificate isn't available to confirm compliance, this will come to light during the purchasers' solicitor investigations, or the buyer's surveyor will flag it up. This can seriously delay things and is likely to worry buyers, even causing the sale to fall through.

You've got Building Regulations approval, but there's no completion certificate
Sometimes there is proof that a Building Regulations application was made for the work, but no completion certificate to show it was satisfactorily completed. In such cases the best course of action is to contact Building Control and arrange a retrospective completion inspection. A new completion certificate can be issued upon satisfactory inspection of the work.

You didn't know that you needed to make a Building Regulations application
Where work has been carried in the past, there may be no record of a Building Regulations application having been made, because the homeowner may have been unaware that it was required. In such cases an application for a 'Regularisation Certificate' can be made. This is basically a retrospective Building Regulations application. But because the work has long been finished, some physical opening up may be necessary to establish that it is structurally sound and confirm compliance. It should be possible to arrange a pre-application inspection so the Building Control team can give you the necessary guidance.

What about indemnity insurance?
Where all else fails, it's sometimes possible to arrange an indemnity insurance policy. Where consent wasn't obtained for the works, paying a premium may allow the sale to proceed by insuring against the risk of a claim. But this is only a short term remedy, affording protection from enforcement action, and the cover may be quite limited. The trouble is, the same problem is likely to arise when future owners come to sell. Also, purchasers can be put off because works that have been carried out illegally could be potentially unsafe. So arranging for the Regularisation documents is always a better option.

8.
Basement Conversions

We've left the subject of extending downwards until last because this tends to be a relatively costly way of adding space to your home. However there is one situation where going underground can sometimes be a very practical solution, and that's where you've already got some form of basement that doesn't require a lot of expensive excavation work.

Many older properties were built with accommodation below ground level. In Georgian and early Victorian townhouses the 'downstairs' was generally utilised for kitchens and occupied by servants. In fact, these are often 'semi-basements' where the ground around the walls has been excavated to form neat trenches with steps leading down from the front garden. Less expensive homes were commonly built with coal cellars under the house, but these tend to be rather cramped with very limited headroom, and hence are impractical for conversion, and better suited to storing wine.

Today, many old basements are unused and neglected, being prone to damp penetration and lacking in natural light and ventilation. But rather than leaving them to fester as redundant space, it's usually possible to overcome the technical challenges and transform them into valuable accommodation, suitable for a range of possible new uses such as kitchen/diners, utility rooms, home offices, dens, gyms or playrooms.

Excavation
Because of the cost and structural upheaval, excavating (or enlarging) basements is generally only worth considering as a last resort once all the other options in this guidebook have been explored, such as extensions and loft conversions. From a financial perspective, digging into the ground underneath the house only really makes sense in densely populated urban areas where there are restrictions on building up or out, and the cost can be justified by the increase in value. Cavernous multi-storey basements are probably best left to multi-millionaire bankers who think nothing of blowing ill-gotten fortunes to create 'iceberg houses'. From a structural perspective, if excavation work isn't carried out with scrupulous care, particularly with fragile older buildings, it can easily result in subsidence and cracking extending to neighbouring properties. Also lowering the floor below the water table level could risk make the property more vulnerable to flooding.

However there are circumstances where making space down below may be a feasible option if the project is professionally planned and executed. However until digging commences there's no way of knowing whether there are hidden problems, so it's advisable to keep a generous contingency fund – and notify your insurers in advance.

Condition

Existing basements built of masonry with no water protection are generally in fairly poor condition. Even some converted basements have struggled to cope with rising groundwater levels caused by record rainfall in recent years because of inadequate water-proofing. So the first job is to assess the condition of the existing structure. Check for signs of damp, ponding water, loose render, and evidence of salt lines and white calcium staining on the walls.

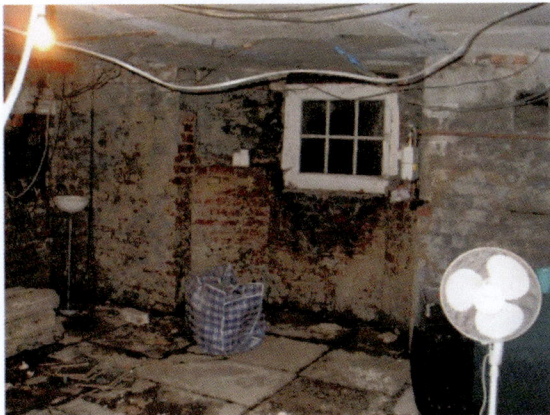

Failure is generally due to groundwater under pressure leaking through cracks, or gaps where new service entry points have been cut into the walls, or faults developing in the waterproofing. But damp is also commonly caused by condensation where ventilation is poor and heating intermittent – or worst of all, where washing machines and tumble dryers are spewing out lots of hot, steamy air! Problems can be made worse where the ground outside has become saturated, due to leaking gutters, blocked gullies and earth or rubbish piled up against the main walls above.

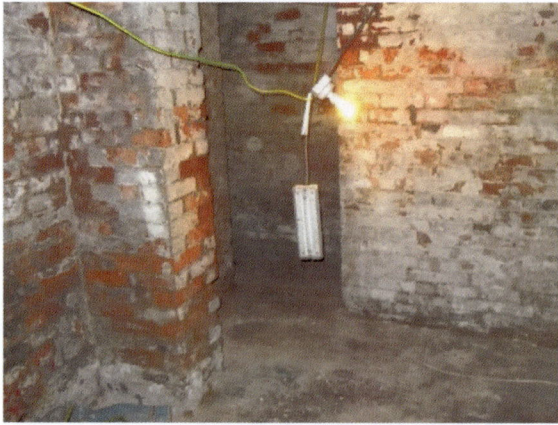

QUESTIONS TO ASK UP FRONT
Before starting some key points need to be checked:-

* Can you convert a basement without planning permission? In most cases the answer is 'yes' – see Permitted Development Rights below. However you will still need to make a Building Regulations application.

* Is my house suitable? Regrettably, the need for expensive and disruptive excavation and underpinning means that in most properties this is not a viable option. Houses with existing basements can be suitable subject to available headroom (bearing in mind that the necessary works to upgrade the floor will eat into the available headroom). But small cellars with low ceilings aren't ideal for conversion.

* What will it cost? In terms of making space on a budget, you can immediately forget any project that's likely to require excavation work because the cost will be outrageously expensive. However upgrading an existing basement can realistic proposition without the need for any major structural work, with costs comparable to building an equivalent extension.

* What does the price include? Basement work is a specialist area and there are firms who offer package deals including a full design service, drawings, structural calculations, and Planning and Building Regs applications. When appointing a contractor it's essential that they are experienced in projects of this type and know exactly what they're doing – so it's well worth taking the trouble to visit some previous basement jobs and talk to the homeowners. Specialist basement conversion firms should cover their work with a warranty backed upby a third party insurance guarantee.

Minimising disturbance
Even with independent access for trades and materials, there will still be a fair amount of noise and vibration emanating from under the reception room floors. So these rooms will need to be vacated during work hours and any priceless ceramics and objets d'art removed from harm's way!

* Access for labour and materials: Fortunately many basements were built with independent access via steps. Or it may be possible to utilise an existing window or lightwell. Excavation via the front garden is often a possibility in properties with ground floors made of traditional suspended timber over a sub floor void, breaking through below ground under the front window. The necessary supporting works, excavation and underpinning can be carried out below the property whilst the occupants carry on living in their home.

* Deliveries: So that building materials can be delivered and safely stored it's a good idea to allocate space in advance.

* Services: The existing electrical and heating systems will normally need to be extended. So schedule a day for this work when the main supply can be temporarily cut off without causing too much disruption.

PLANNING & BUILDING REGS

Planning consent is not normally needed for straightforward conversions of existing basements. However it will be required in cases where the works alter the external appearance of the property, such as where a lightwell or new window is added, and also where major excavation work is needed to enlarge or create a new basement. However from a planning perspective this can be something of a 'grey area', and can vary depending on the local Planning Authority. However, if you want to change the use of the building in some way, e.g. by using the basement as a separate self-contained flat, a planning application will be necessary. And of course changes to Listed buildings always need consent.

When it comes to the Building Regulations, the works will need to comply in a number of key areas listed below. These are discussed in more detail later under 'Design Matters'.

    * Waterproofing
    * Structure
    * Access and means of escape from fire
    * Ground floor fire resistance
    * Ventilation & condensation
    * Stairs
    * Thermal insulation
    * Electrics
    * Light
    * Headroom
    * Potential risk of flooding
    * Radon

Party walls
For any excavation work within 3 metres of your neighbour's house, or any work directly affecting party walls, the Party Wall Act will apply (mainly relevant for terraces and semi-detached houses). To

help smooth things along it's a good idea to reassure the neighbours well in advance, before they hear about your proposals from from Party Wall Surveyor or the Planners.

Conversion Methods

There are a number of methods used to damp-proof and convert basements. 'Tanking' is probably the best known approach, where traditionally waterproof render would be applied directly to the walls and floor to seal them. But today this is generally considered to be the least effective system. Modern 'drained cavity systems' use special dimpled plastic sheets as water-impervious linings, sandwiched between the basement walls and a new interior wall. There are a number of variations on this theme.

Whichever conversion method you select, before starting work it makes sense to reduce the amount of water trying to get into the basement from outside. So the first job is to fix leaking gutters etc that are causing the ground to become saturated. Where the water table is higher than the basement floor it may be necessary to install an external land drain.

Drained cavity systems

Basement conversions with drained cavities allow any groundwater that gets into the basement to be safely channelled, collected and discharged. Water can be removed using a gravity-fed drainage system, or by pumping it away from a sump.

Ventilated dry lining systems work by isolating the original wall surfaces behind a new lining, then building a new inner wall, leaving a ventilated air gap in between. This is achieved by lining the basement walls in giant sheets of 'bubble wrap' (a textured polyethylene membrane). These are fixed to wall surfaces using sealed fixing plugs designed to accommodate a certain amount of dampness in basement walls. A new independent interior wall is then constructed as an inner leaf, e.g. of protected timber studwork. This new wall is lined with a vapour barrier and fully insulated to inhibit condensation, before plasterboarding on the room side. To the floor, a screed is laid over a damp proof membrane (DPM). Where space is at a premium, it may be possible to use special thin latex screeds and floor finishes.

In basements where damp is likely to be more excessive, a more robust solution involves building a new 'room within the room' by constructing new blockwork walls and floor which are isolated from the main structure by DPMs and a drained cavity.

The key component is the facility to collect and drain or pump away water from the cavity (or below the new floor screed). Drainage channels, a sump and a submersible electric pump can be used if there is no surface water drain at basement level.

DESIGN MATTERS

Basement accommodation can be suitable for a number of possible uses. However, they are not ideally suited for use as bedrooms because of the noise from hallways and living rooms above, plus the limited light and ventilation. But whatever the proposed use, particular care is needed with the design of damp-proofing, stairs, fire exits, natural light, and drainage.

Structure

Where the existing floor levels in basements need to be lowered, it's essential that the foundations are not undermined by excavation work. In older buildings disturbance to the structure can be especially damaging, particularly in terraced houses, which of course have shared party walls. So a structural engineer will need to advise, and the design approved in advance by Building Control. All structural work including excavation and underpinning of walls should be carried out by a fully insured specialist firm.

Light

Natural light is often very restricted in basements. One possible solution is to excavate small external lightwells which can channel light down to windows.

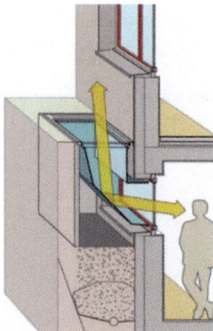

These act as small 'shafts' (or wells) that allow light to pass downwards from above, and can be protected on top with special glazing or a grille covering at ground level. Alternatively, to prevent people falling into the well guarding should be provided (1100mm high and non-climbable). It might also be worth exploring the use of 'light tubes'.

As well as natural light, designing the optimum style of artificial lighting is important, and downlighters can be particularly effective for lighting basement rooms.

Stair access

If there are no existing stairs down to the basement, or just some inadequate beetle infested steps, a new flight of stairs will need to be installed. The standard requirement for new stairs is a pitch no steeper than 42 degrees, with 2 metres headroom, and suitable handrails at least 900mm high(and spindles no further apart than 100mm). Also the rise in height between each step should not exceed 220mm, and each step (the 'going') should be at least 220mm deep.

Smoke alarms

Mains operated and interlinked smoke detectors should be provided to the ground floor hallway and first floor landing, as well as to the basement (in 3 or storey or higher buildings smoke alarms are needs at all levels).

Means of escape in case of fire

To comply with Fire Regulations habitable basements need some form of safe exit to allow occupants to escape in the event of a fire. There are a number of ways this can be achieved:-

* The ideal solution is where a basement has already got a suitable door or window providing access to outside. To qualify as an 'escape window' it needs to have a clear opening of at least 0.33m², with the height and width no less than 450mm; also the bottom of the window should be not higher than 1100mm above the floor. The window should be fitted with special fire-escape hinges (ensuring it can be fully opened). Having escaped through the window, people then need to safely reach ground level, so in some cases steps may need to be provided leading out to the garden.

* If your basement has an external lightwell, it may be possible to upgrade it to provide a secondary fire escape (as well as light and ventilation). In the event of a fire, the occupants should be able to climb through a suitably sized window into the lightwell and then up to the garden. So a short ladder may need to be fitted into the wall of the lightwell. Where there's a grille covering on top, it may be possible to fit a hatch within the grille through which you can escape.

* If the basement does not have a suitable window or door leading to the outside, then you will need to provide a fire-protected escape route leading from the basement to a main 'final exit door' from the building (e.g. the front or back door). This is a similar requirement to loft conversions. The good news is, where the basement is accessed from the house by a door leading down from the hallway, with a bit of modification the existing entrance hall will normally suffice. The basement door will need to be upgraded to a fire door of minimum 20 minutes fire rating (FD20). In addition, all the other doors opening onto the hallway at ground floor level will need to be similarly upgraded to fire doors (FD20).

* Where the basement is accessed from the house by a door leading down from a room such as a kitchen (as opposed to a hallway) the following solution can be applied. At the top of the basement stairs a small lobby can be constructed (of fire-resisting materials) with 2 separate fire doors. Each door should leading in opposite directions allowing escape to outside.

* If properties of 3 or more storeys before the basement conversion, fire doors are required at all levels to all habitable rooms that open onto the stairs.

These solutions assume the new basement accommodation comprises a single habitable room (plus perhaps an en-suite or utility).

The floor above

In many basements the joists and floor above will be exposed. Even where there are ceilings these tend to be damp and in need replacement. So a new sheets of plasterboard will need to be applied to the joists, comprising a double layer of 12.5mm plasterboard (ideally of the pink coloured fire-board type) with a skim plaster finish. First however the space between the joists should be packed with sound-proofing insulation, e.g. with 100mm of mineral wool quilt. Note that where the basement only occupies part of the space under the ground floor, there may be an adjacent suspended timber floor and adequate ventilation must be maintained to the sub-floor void.

Ventilation
Any new habitable room will need to be properly ventilated. Opening windows, perhaps via lightwells, can provide sufficient 'rapid ventilation'. Specifically the requirement is for an opening window equivalent to 1/20th of the floor area of the room. You also need to provide controllable background ventilation, such as from tickle vents in door and window frames (8000mm² for habitable rooms and 4000mm² for kitchens, bathrooms and utility rooms). Where natural ventilation through windows is not practical, a mechanical ventilation system will need to be installed, so the design will need to accommodate the necessary ducting. Also in any bathroom, shower room, utility or kitchen, extractor fans must be fitted to expel humid air to outside (usually linked to light switches).

Thermal insulation

A reasonable thickness of insulation should be provided to the existing walls and floor, meeting current new build standards where practicable. The insulating material must be compatible with the tanking material. New windows and doors should meet U-value standard of 1.6 Wm²/k (e.g. 'low E' argon or krypton filled).

Heating
One of the benefits of basement rooms is that, being enclosed by the ground, room temperatures tend to be reasonably warm in winter and cool in summer. However, some form of heating will still be required, usually by extending the existing central heating systems with an extra radiator or two, assuming it's up to the job. Alternatively, where headroom permits, installing UFH can provide a more efficient solution.

Drainage
If you plan to include a bathroom, cloakroom, kitchen or utility, the drainage connections will need to be considered at an early stage. Waste water from new sinks, basins, baths, showers and appliances such as washing machines and dishwashers will need to connect to the foul drains, not the rainwater system. In fact in most areas it's illegal to connect to make 'misconnections' by mixing up relatively clean surface water (from rain) and waste from bathrooms and kitchens. So when planning layouts make sure there are suitable routes for pipe runs. In deeper rooms you may not be able to rely on

gravity to disperse waste water, so a pumped system may be needed to connect with the main drainage system. Where space is limited, new WCs can sometimes be fitted with electrically powered macerators which facilitate the use of narrow bore pipes.

Electrical installations

New electrical circuits for power and lighting will need to be installed, plus additional circuits for any new kitchens and showers etc. If your existing system is reasonably modern it may have spare capacity at the consumer unit to accommodate the increased loadings. Installation must be carried out either by a registered self-certifying electrician or by a 'competent person' (i.e. an electrician who can issue an electrical installation certificate under BS7671). If the consumer unit is located in the basement it will need to be moved from the wall to allow for the conversion works. New lighting must be energy efficient, preferable LEDs.

HAPPY ENDINGS

Hopefully this guide has been useful in exploring the different options for adding more space to your home. So now for the tough part - picking the one that suits for your property - and your wallet!

Apart form the 8 main ways of making more space covered in this guide, there may be other possibilities – for example a tree house could perhaps be a brilliant new playroom for the kids. Or it might be possible to 'mix and match' some of the projects we've looked at in this guide, for example a new underground basement room in the back garden (basically a swimming pool with a roof!).

If you decide to go ahead with a major project such as an extension or loft conversion, it's worth investing in a detailed 'step-by-step' guide, such as the Haynes Home Extension Manual or Loft Conversion Manual.

Of course you may ultimately decide not to extend or convert, and instead focus on renovating your home, transforming it into a super new living space, without blowing the budget. But whichever route you take we hope the information in these pages has been of help - and we wish you the very best of luck!

Useful websites

Planningportal.gov.uk

Rightsurvey.co.uk

Home-extension.com

Loft-rooms.com

Home-insulating.com

The End

Printed in Great Britain
by Amazon

85921593R00060